Risk Reconsidered

Printed in the United States of America
First edition: July 2018
Tautegory Press, Seattle, Washington USA

Printing History
The original articles were all first published by *The Risk Universe* magazine, London, England; and by *ASA News & Notes*. Permission has been granted for this reprint.

USA Library of Congress Control Number: 2018907913
ISBN: 978-0-9839347-9-0

Cover and Interior Design: Marie Williams Chant

Risk Reconsidered

Annie Searle

ASA Institute for Risk & Innovation

TAUTEGORY PRESS
SEATTLE, WASHINGTON

Introduction

I lead at least three lives. As principal of Annie Searle & Associates LLC, I consult and speak around the country on operational risk issues that arise in both the public and the private sector. As a faculty lecturer in the University of Washington's Information School, I teach the history of risk and analyze current events in the context of methodologies and frameworks. As an author, I write and publish on topics as esoteric as personal risk, privacy, cybersecurity, terrorism, third party risk, crisis management and information ethics.

This past summer, I found time to reconsider a body of work that is neither fish nor fowl. Written over five years (2012-2017), the twenty articles were published in the London-based magazine, *The Risk Universe*, usually within a week of having been written. By and large they are focused on the world as I found it at any given point in time. Initially, I thought that would limit their usefulness because of the time that has passed. Upon review, I believe most of them hold up very well. I should like to thank Mike Finlay, publisher of *The Risk Universe*, for permission to reprint these articles; and, at the same time, thank the two editors I worked with at the magazine: Victoria Tozer-Pennington and Carrie Cook.

To make this book more useful, I have added head notes to each of the articles, referencing the larger risk issue or framework in which it fits.

I have also added an addendum to the volume, consisting of ten columns I wrote for *ASA News & Notes* that focus primarily on the geopolitical risk and actual damage done by the current U.S. administration since 2017 to our democracy.

Seattle, 2018

Table of Contents

Table of Contents

Reflections on the lost bank
Issue 7, July 2012

As a senior executive reporting at the end to both the chief information officer and the chief market risk officer at Washington Mutual Bank, I had a front row seat for the largest bank failure in American history as well as the reverberations felt across the large banks when the federal government stepped in to shore them up via Troubled Asset Relief Program (TARP) funds. But that didn't happen until after Washington Mutual Bank had been seized by FDIC regulators on September 26, 2008 and sold immediately to JPMorgan Chase at fire sale pricing. To this day I ask myself how I could not have known that we were at the cliff's edge. My first clue came when the CIO said no to a summer scenario test that the crisis management team wanted to schedule: that scenario was a hypothetical "run on bank" by depositors rushing to remove their funds. The CIO felt that the scenario would cause participants to believe it was real. But in fact it began to be real later in the summer, when I learned the FDIC had been monitoring our daily cash deposit/withdrawal flows. My second clue came directly from the CEO. He and I had ridden together in an empty elevator in early September, and I asked him if there were not a way he could send an uplifting message to employees in what was a grim, anxious environment with the failures of Bear Stearns in August and Lehman Brothers on September 15 – his answer was legalistic in the extreme, that he could only say to me or to all employees what he said to the shareholders. He was removed and replaced by the board of directors on September 8. I should have realized at either of those points that we had entered the underworld, but like my peers, I was not looking at outliers. I was trying to do my job in an anxious environment and hold my own teams together. I was so confident that we would come out the other side that I moved a chunk of my deferred compensation into Washington Mutual stock. Not even a new CEO, who understood the politics of regulation that prevails still in the Wall Street-Washington DC corridor of power, could save the bank. He was just flying back to

Seattle from intensive meetings with regulators and congressional representatives when the FDIC walked in to shut us down

Since that time, the 2007-2008 financial crisis has been the focus of significant research, including a 2009 RIMS white paper on whether or not risk management professionals dropped the ball. The authors conclude that the practice of risk management was, at that time, so new that there was no playbook. I find little solace in that determination.

In this article, I review both the book, The Lost Bank *and add my own thoughts on the extent to which the failure of Washington Mutual was due to a kind of reckless disregard for operational risk flags that presented themselves years before the FDIC moved in to seize the bank and sell it to JPMorgan Chase. I use the four Basel risk lenses to perform the analysis: people, process, systems and/or outside events.*

Certainly the financial crisis led to improved practices at most large banks, with the advent of heightened scrutiny from regulators as well as provisions in the Dodd Frank Act designed to keep large banks from failing at the taxpayers' expense. A glaring exception today is to be found at Wells Fargo, the nation's third largest bank in 2018, whom I write about more extensively in another article in this volume. Elsewhere in the world, we have seen very large banks like Deutsche struggle with fines and regulatory breaches, despite a series of continuing losses.

At the CEO level, Wells Fargo, Deutsche Bank and Goldman Sachs have or will anoint new CEOs, while the most successful CEOs who bridged the financial crisis – Jamie Dimon at JPMorgan Chase and Brian T. Moynihan at Bank of America -- remain in place. Subsequent articles in this volume look at the characteristics of a leader who can manage both up to the board of directors and down to senior management and thousands of employees who interact with customers every day.

Kristen Grind's book, *The Lost Bank: The Story of Washington Mutual – The Biggest Bank Failure in American History* (Simon & Schuster, 389pp, $27.00) is an important and revealing study with implications beyond its central subject. Rather than focusing on the larger economic meltdown in 2008, Grind's book examines how Washington Mutual's strategy, culture and risk appetite underwent a significant change over 20+ years, as it moved from a regional thrift, to seeing itself as having the potential to become what was called a "category killer."[1] Against the larger story of the bank, Grind describes the metamorphosis of Kerry Killinger, from a smart, ambitious but grounded financial analyst to chairman and CEO of what would become the nation's seventh largest bank.

Grind's book is well researched and footnoted, with hundreds of interviews, close readings of annual reports, lawsuits and the 2010 Senate Investigations Subcommittee hearings on Washington Mutual. Grind provides context for the earlier days of the bank, focusing in particular on the period when lawyer Lou Pepper became CEO and hired a number of smart people, including Killinger, a securities analyst with a small investment firm that Washington Mutual acquired in 1982, who did not at that time have a banking background. Six years later, Pepper and the Washington Mutual board selected Killinger as his successor to run the bank.

The first two chapters of *The Lost Bank* provide historical context for the Pepper years between 1981 and 1988, which stabilised the 1889 savings and loan institution. Grind's description of those years includes reflections from some of the participants of the team that Pepper assembled, as well as from Pepper himself. There are characterizations of some of the folksier "friend of the family" brand elements of that culture – dressing up for Halloween, holiday parties, executives performing skits in the lobby – with less attention paid by Grind to the civic and cultural contributions that Washington Mutual made and of which many former bank employees are still proud.

The bank encouraged its employees to make diverse personal contributions to charitable organisations, by offering various levels of annual match. It regularly underwrote community events in key locations across the country. Washington Mutual "had donated $50 million annually to organizations involved with affordable housing, community building and education, including cash grants to schools in 15 states; $8 million a year has gone to 250 nonprofit and civic groups in the Seattle area alone."[2] Though the bank had begun to grow, the culture of the 1990s and early 2000s aligned with its traditional values of "fair, caring and human". Teamwork was highly valued and Killinger's own "check your ego at the door" was still the mantra.

Having accomplished large and successful mergers on the retail bank side in the 1990s, it's not surprising that Washington Mutual's values grew from three – "fair, caring and human"– to five – add "dynamic and driven" – when it began to acquire additional home loans companies as part of its growth strategy. Marketing for the retail bank and home loans divisions was handled within each silo, but with a playful emphasis on customer service and ease of use. As if to prove that unstuffy non-bank image, the bank's name contracted, from "Washington Mutual" to "WaMu" in 2007.

Using an operational risk assessment approach, and to amplify Grind's own findings, I have mapped her book to an operational risk failure grid that looks at how the intersection of people, process, systems and external events often lead to financial loss without proper risk management.

People: There was no one person who brought down Washington Mutual. It was a culture change that began when the bank incorporated officers accustomed to other corporate values, particularly from acquired organisations. The strategy shifted from acquisition of retail banks that expanded the branch footprint and deposits, to the acquisition of banks with home loans platforms. Grind describes how home loans executive Craig Davis brought in a group of his former subordinates from American Savings Bank who were added to the mix, along with managers and staff kept as a result of this and other acquisitions.[3] Grind notes, that at the same time Davis was elevated to head of the home loans group, "he [Killinger] announced bold plans to grab 20 per cent of the nationwide mortgage market share, more than four times the amount Washington had held in 2000."[4]

I recall that the theme for the 2000 "State of the Group" annual meeting was "Running with the Big Dogs." Toward that end, Killinger introduced the company's new Human Relations (HR) executive to lead recruiting efforts and to develop an updated compensation plan, with leadership training programs that would further put everyone on the same strategic and cultural page. The drive to modernise technology led to the hiring of an Australian bank CIO, who understood the mortgage market from his time at Countrywide. Grind describes how additional hires were made at the executive level from respectable institutions like General Electric and JPMorgan Chase.[5] Though he may have been pressured earlier by the board of directors and by the leadership development books popular at that time, Killinger took until 2004 to decide upon a COO, perhaps realising he would lose his close oversight of the executive team. As Grind notes, Steve Rotella was ready to leave JPMorgan Chase when it was acquired by Bank One and Jamie Dimon moved into the President & COO position in 2004.[6] When he chose Rotella from JPMorgan Chase in 2004 over the two key executives who had served him well through acquisitions and cleanups, they left the bank. Once Rotella was in place, there was very little left of the original executive team that Lou Pepper had put together. Both Bill Longbrake (CFO then CRO) and Craig Tall (Executive Vice President for Corporate Development) had been moved off the executive team to advisory roles that same year.[7] Now the heads of all the business units, as well as technology, reported to Rotella, a key point I think that could have been examined in more detail in Grind's book.

Process: The single greatest change to organisational processes, especially at the executive level occurred when Killinger "divided Washington Mutual into three different units, or silos, making each silo its own autonomous business. While some of those people remained in leadership positions, the new structure effectively wiped out the cohesion of the team, long a factor in Washington Mutual's success."[8] Each of the three groups maintained their own office and branch infrastructure for some years, as if to reinforce the silos. In building out an enterprise level risk scorecard for the company, the project team found a lack of documentation around business processes within and across the silos that Grind describes. From my own experience, I know that the only repository companywide that the scorecard project team later found was in the Office of Continuity Assurance, where each business unit had to describe in detail how the work got done so that a workaround plan could be prepared in case of disasters. Unfortunately, the bank had not developed or tested a plan that would handle runs on banks by its depositors of the type that Grind painstakingly documents in Chapter 9 of the book.

Systems: Though efforts began in 2001 to clean up the bank's multiple business applications and upgrade its hardware platforms, the side effects of multiple acquisitions showed up most clearly in the spaghetti-like schematics of the bank's technology architecture. Streamlining could only be performed if banking units were sure that moving their application would not in any way jeopardise its operation or if the technology costs were too high. I recall that the regulators expressed concerns over home loans financial results because the group was operating, at one point, with at least a dozen different lending platforms. In 2000 the Home Loans Group undertook, and later wrote down and off the development of, its own proprietary home loans platform, called Optis, contracting the work to the California firm Accenture. Grind points again to the perils of silos: "Because the Home Loans Group had ownership of the project and it was carried out within that silo of the bank, some WaMu managers and executives didn't know the extent of the problems. Others who offered help were turned away."[9] It was hard to resist the power points – Optis looked like a dream machine that would also put a feather in the cap of the technology group. From at least my perspective, a great deal of what would become the "think big" behavior that later became reckless risk-taking started here. As a 2004 CNN article pointed out, Washington Mutual lost ground to competitors because "Optis worked well for processing mortgage applications, but it failed in the far more important tasks of processing, underwriting and closing the loans."[10]

External Events: In a fine irony, Killinger had prophesised the bank's demise in 2003 when he said that "We hope to do to this industry what Wal-Mart did to theirs, Starbucks to theirs, Costco did to theirs and Lowe's-Home Depot did to their industry. And I think if we've done our job, five years from now you're not going to call us a bank."[11] Five years later, a version of his prophesy came true.

In a letter to friends and family written after Grind's book was published, subsequently reported in the *New York Times*, Killinger lays out what he perceives to be major inaccuracies in *The Lost Bank*. After detailing measures that the board and management took to reduce home loans from 2003 to 2007, and to raise new capital in 2007-2008, Killinger expresses his view that the book "largely misses the point that most sophisticated participants in the financial industry failed to accurately predict – the extent of the national housing downturn. Any fair recounting of the financial crisis would note that any errors made in failing to anticipate the severity of the housing collapse were made collectively by the entire financial industry and the government. It is a gross understatement to say that I am greatly saddened that the company is not here today and that it was not provided the many benefits and programs that were so beneficial to large Wall Street banks when the financial crisis reached its peak."[12]

Roger Lowenstein's excellent book, *The End of Wall Street*, provides a full characterisation of that entire environment, as Killinger suggests Grind's does not, but he cannot be much happier with his portrayal in that book. Lowenstein suggests that as early as 2005, "With success coming so easily, WaMu was deaf to the need to monitor its risk" and as early as that same year "…with Killinger, the rising tide of risk tolerance loosened his moorings."[13]

Clearly the leaders at Washington Mutual seemed unable to course correct the growth strategy and dial down their exposure, even though all the key risk indicators were there as early as late 2006. In the long run, we have to ask why the strong bench that had been assembled couldn't see it coming. Several former chief risk officers had raised questions on the housing bubble and on subprime mortgages as early as 2003. Bill Longbrake had been writing and presenting reports to the board of directors for some years that included "a macro view of the economy and the housing market,"[14] Jim Vanasek, who had built a pristine credit history for the company as its chief credit officer succeeded Longbrake as chief risk officer, but retired in 2005 once it was clear that both Killinger and the board of directors were deaf to his arguments.[15] Yet large firms like JPMorgan Chase and Goldman Sachs had begun to significantly reduce their exposure to risk from other banks and to the subprime mortgage business late in 2006. Washington Mutual rejected JPMorgan Chase's offer of $8 per share in March of 2008, thinking the bank had sufficient capital after a new infusion to see it through the bottom of the mortgage crisis. As runs on the bank began to erode its liquidity and as various ratings downgrades occurred, executives at Washington Mutual continued to believe that things were going to turn around. Books like Lowenstein's document the chaos in other parts of the economic environment of 2008: Fannie and Freddie and AIG had been propped up or bailed out; Lehman had failed; Bear Stearns was acquired at fire sale prices by JPMorgan Chase and now the FDIC was letting other banks know that Washington Mutual would soon be available for bid. Lowenstein characterises this period in a few sentences: "During the third week of September, the week of the TARP debate, all went silent. WaMu could not figure out why its calls to suitors were going unanswered. The reason was that the federal regulators had preempted the auction."[16] It was too late, despite efforts by Alan Fishman, the East Coast CEO hired that month to replace Killinger. Banks strong enough to consider making the acquisition were waiting to see when the sale would begin. From Grind, describing Sheila Bair's later testimony, "In the FDIC's view, WaMu's closure was a success. Not a dime of the deposit insurance fund had been used in connection with the largest bank failure in US history. The government isn't charged with protecting bank shareholders or employees. Its job is to protect customers."[17]

Shareholders who have never worked in a financial institution will read Grind's book at one level, while those of us who were there will be hanging on the edges of our seats beginning with Chapter 7, "Scenes from the Great Depression," which begins with the 2008 annual meeting for shareholders. From this point on, Grind takes us inside the action, where in Chapter 9, "The Final Hours," we are shown Washington Mutual's net deposit balances day by day from September 8 onwards. In the epilogue to the book, where Grind amplifies on how little noticed was the failure of Washington Mutual in the larger context of the economic collapse, she notes of Killinger's Congressional testimony in 2010 that "former executives and managers of WaMu watched the congressional grilling, thinking nothing unusual of Killinger's responses. It was entirely possible, they believed, that Killinger didn't know what was happening. He had continued to believe that the risks the bank took could be managed. He couldn't see how his strategy decisions, made at the highest level of the company, had created a poisonous lending culture at the bottom."[18]

Certainly the executive team felt that there was sufficient liquidity to weather the September run on the bank even as it tried to entertain potential buyers. They might have been right, especially with a new CEO who had the right Wall Street and Washington D.C. connections – except that Washington Mutual had never developed the so-called fifth line of business[19] that would provide it with strong government support at such a critical time. Both the OTS and the FDIC regulated Washington Mutual, with the OTS consistently backing off the FDIC. The infighting and highly divergent views of the two regulators on the health of the bank should have been sufficient tip to prepare and mobilise an actionable public sector strategy. While the bank did have a relatively small government relations team in Washington D.C., it was focused primarily on Capitol Hill. A Washington Mutual senior liaison that functioned at the level of Secretary Paulson and his direct reports at Treasury and who enjoyed their confidence as well as the confidence of Sheila Bair might have made all the difference in the final decision-making. But this is not the type of strategy or relationship that can be built overnight. As it was, Bair characterised Washington Mutual's failure as "barely a blip given everything else that was going on."[20] In a culture of inflated confidence around growth, especially in the years 2000-2007, it might be hard to believe that Washington Bank would ever need the government at its back to survive. JPMorgan Chase's Jamie Dimon had early on cultivated those close relationships with high government officials that Washington Mutual had not managed. As Grind's book makes clear, by the time Washington Mutual's new CEO, Alan Fishman, got to Washington D.C. to make the rounds among all the agencies and departments, the decision on the bank's future had already been made. In *Last Man Standing*, Jamie Dimon discusses the two fire sale acquisitions that JPMorgan Chase made back to back in 2008, when the government turned to him as a trusted partner, "the nation's bank," in the midst of the economic meltdown that drove fear through the markets and the regulators alike: "Bear was never a home run, but WaMu will prove to be a great thing for the company over the long run."[21]

References

1. Kristen Grind, *The Lost Bank: The Story of Washington Mutual – The Biggest Bank Failure in American History* (New York: Simon & Schuster, 2012), p. 91.

2. PBS Newshour, "Amid Financial Crisis, WaMu Collapse Hits Hard in Seattle," October 15, 2008.

3. Grind, pp. 67-68.

4. Grind, p. 67.

5. Grind, pp. 98-99.

6. Grind, p. 105.

7. Grind, pp. 97-98.

8. Ibid.

9. Grind, p. 100-101.

10. Shawn Tully, "What Went Wrong at WaMu," *CNNMoney*, August 9, 2004.

11. Peter S. Goodman and Gretchen Morgenson, "Saying Yes to Anyone, WaMu Built Empire on Shaky Loans," *New York Times*, December 28, 2008.

12. William Alden, Washington Mutual's Former Chief Takes Issue With Book's Portrayal," *New York Times*, June 21, 2012.

13. Roger Lowenstein, *The End of Wall Street* (Penguin: New York, 2010, 2011), pages 33 and 36.

14. Grind, p.162.

15. Grind, pp. 149-150.

16. Lowenstein, p 239.

17. Grind, p. 315.

18. Grind, p. 330.

19. JPMorgan Chase has been said to have a "seventh line of business" which is public sector lobbying and advocacy both at the Treasury Department and Congressional level

20. Grind, p. 314.

21. Duff McDonald, *Last Man Standing* (New York: Simon & Schuster, 2009), p.307.

Ethical misconduct: Is it your biggest risk?
Issue 11, November 2012

Examining both the causes and the risk that arise from misconduct in the workplace has been a longstanding focus of my work. A company's culture is formed out of whether or not employees believe in the "tone at the top" from the board of directors and executive leadership. Employees are far more likely to imitate the behavior of their leaders, or to see that behavior as an enabler of misconduct, than they are to align themselves with the company's written code of conduct.

The list of CEOs who left their company under the cloud of misconduct in this article covers only 2008 to 2012, to which we could easily add more recent instances like that of Travis Kalanick from Uber, Richard Smith from Equifax, Steve Ellis at Chipotle; and John Stumpf from Wells Fargo. A recent study by PwC indicates that CEO dismissals for ethical misconduct rose 36% for the five year period ending 2016 over the previous five years. The proposals I make at the end of this article to reduce ethical misconduct are as applicable today as they were in 2012.

The most flagrant example of misconduct that continues on despite additional regulation and fines is Wells Fargo, whose most recent fines include a one billion dollar fine from the Consumer Financial Protection Bureau for abuses in its auto loan and mortgage interest rate business lines. This large fine comes less than two years after an almost $200 million fine for opening fake deposit and credit card accounts. Despite a recent double page advertisement in the New York Times *on May 6, 2018 asking for customers' trust and new business, one wonders how the culture will actually be fixed without replacement of the current CEO at Wells, himself an internal promotion.*

I owned a computer hardware company for 15 years, and one of my earliest writing projects was the creation of an employee handbook that outlined issues that ranged from dress code to values and acceptable behaviour. My experience of owning and operating the company offered direct, hands-on operational risk management for both myself and our customers. My ten years of experience at Washington Mutual offered a wider pathway to an understanding of all types on internal controls that are at the heart of enterprise risk management, as well as some brutal lessons on just how difficult it is to manage risk when a company is siloed and when executives cast a blind eye in order to obtain profits. My subsequent work as a consultant for critical infrastructure companies has broadened my understanding of regulations and controls in both the public and private sector: operational risk management must be married to the strategic planning process if it is to be truly effective.

I subscribe to Basel's understanding of the factors that can lead to financial loss – people, processes, systems, and external events. Of all four, from at least what I have seen, people are at the heart of operational risk management, whether policies and programs are in effect or not. And that gets us back to a discussion of values and behaviour.

Ethics are the moral principles of right and wrong that govern conduct and illuminate character. One's character is defined by one's values. Our values and some patterns of behaviour are formed early. How old were you when a parent or teacher said "Honesty is the best policy?" How old were you when you first heard the Golden Rule: "Do unto others as you would have done unto you?" For business author Robert Maxwell, it's the Golden Rule that asks "How would I like to be treated in this situation?" He believes that question is as valid in business as it is in private life, that there should be no distinction between personal and business ethics (John C. Maxwell, *There's No Such Thing as "Business" Ethics*. New York: Warner Business Books, 2003). For the philosopher Immanuel Kant, it boils down to what Kant called the principle of publicity: "Could you stand the heat if this were made public?" Kant's question is strikingly similar to one of the filters that Nordstrom CEO Blake Nordstrom says the company applies when making a complex decision involving customer, culture and reputation: "would it put us on '60 Minutes?'" (for those not familiar with the American television program, it is not a program on which most companies wish to appear, since its focus is primarily investigative, shedding light on unethical or fraudulent business practices).

For many of us, ethics can be equated with doing what we say, with mirroring in our behaviour the values we espouse. In today's business environment, that can be trickier than we think. Moral trade-offs seem sometimes to have become the norm.

Here's a selected list of CEOs removed from their positions for one or more of the seven categories of Basel risk:

> **2008** *Board member and former McKinsey CEO Raj Gupta (insider trading)*
> **2010** *British Petroleum CEO Tony Hayward (external event)*
> **2010** *Hewlett Packard CEO Mark Hurd (falsifying reports)*
> **2012** *Highmark CEO Kenneth Melani (junior employee)*
> **2012** *Best Buy CEO Brian Dunn (personal misconduct)*
> **2010** *Lotus CEO Dany Bahar (financial mismanagement)*

What I understand least is how any of these CEOs did not understand Kant's principle of publicity: how did they think they would not be caught? Did they feel they were above the controls structure? On one hand, they seemed to understand how powerful they were – if they understood that, then why behave so foolishly as to get caught. Of this list, only Raj Gupta will to go jail in addition to paying a large fine.

In our consulting practice, one of the first pieces of due diligence we perform is to discover whether or not a code of ethics is in place, and well-understood by employees; and whether new employees receive an orientation on corporate values and ethical behaviour.

The Risk Universe has devoted more column inches than any other publication to human behaviour and operational risk questions. In particular, the "Unethical and illegal practices rife, says survey" article (*The Risk Universe*, July 2012) that focused on the Labaton Sucharow study and the "Whistleblowing retaliation is rising" article (*The Risk Universe*, September 2012) indicate clearly that we are not on the same page where ethical conduct is concerned; and that without some new type of training, we should decrease our expectations that employees or executives will "do the right thing."

A new study shows how much better companies perform financially when they have focused programs to identify unethical behaviour and correct it. The Corporate Executive Board (CEB) RiskClarity Corporate Integrity Service shows that, on ten-year shareholder returns, higher integrity companies outperform others by 16.2%. Over 525,000 employees at 130 companies have participated in this survey that identifies seven attributes that affect corporate culture, like tone at the top, openness of communications and organisational justice.

What specific, practical steps can be taken to improve internal programs and reduce ethical misconduct?

1. Review the corporate values/vision statement
Is it a marketing slogan, directed at customers and investors, or is it a statement of values, written to be intelligible to employees and pointing to desirable behaviour? Companies like Nordstrom and Starbucks have embedded their corporate values in front line employee behaviour.

2. Create/Review the code of conduct
Sometime ethics boils down to deciding what to do when there isn't an absolute rule or regulation. Sometimes ethics boils down to reporting misconduct rather than taking the low road. Simply following the regulations sets a very low bar. Use the values statement and the code of conduct to put a real communications program together that uses examples of appropriate and inappropriate behaviour. Make it more than a one-time orientation with an annual online check-in.

3. Incent employees to do the right thing
Recognise exemplary conduct. Storytelling is an effective way to make the ethical point – find employees who did the right thing even when there was no specific rule to follow or someone watching. Periodically recognise teams who perform well. Include ethical conduct as a percentage of bonus annually, either at the individual or group level. And be sure that HR

profiles managers inclined to retaliate against employees who report misconduct. If they cannot correct their own retaliatory behaviour, they should not be managing people.

4. Build a fraud and misconduct plan
Conduct a misconduct risk assessment. Identify weaknesses and create a mitigation plan as well as a response team. Train employees on how to report misconduct or fraud by identifying what it is. Develop a program that includes triggers to move a report from an "allegation" to an "investigation." Make clear to staff and managers that retaliation from reporting is unacceptable in every way.

5. Create your own program
The revised SEC whistleblower program assumes that with stronger cash incentives, there will be a higher level of participation. But why not create your own program and reduce your own reputational risk directly? An internal whistleblower program that guarantees anonymity, employment protection and a monetary award is a best practice. Consider also what I call, for lack of a better term, an "I Made A Mistake" program that allows employees to self-report unethical decisions or behaviour without being punished or retaliated against. I believe there could be a lot of room here for building such a program's requirements and scope. It is worth considering, even if the first year only brings reports of pilfered office supplies. If you deploy online training, then use lots of scenarios and multiple choice options.

6. Ask your senior leaders to reinforce ethical conduct verbally and with their own performances
If your leaders aren't behaving in an exemplary fashion and modeling the behaviour they wish to see from employees, it's hard for employees to take ethics issues seriously. In this respect, misconduct by leaders could include cutting corners, manufacturing data, waiving requirements or eliminating critical risk practices.

It is fear that drives employees to misconduct – aggrievement that they are not appreciated, fear that they will not get their bonus, fear that they will not be promoted, fear that they will not have enough money, and, in today's climate, fear that they will be fired. As a leader, what else can you do? Above all, you can create a climate for your team to ensure that members are not afraid to give you bad news. You can learn to say "I was wrong" and "thanks for your insight." This is not exactly the same as ensuring that you never retaliate against an employee who reports misconduct, but it is close. To succeed as a leader yourself, you need to remove as many of these fears as you can, to unleash as much productivity as possible, and to make it possible, through the climate you create for employees, to take well managed risks that will pay off for the company.

Perfect pitch: Writing for Executives
Issue 15, March 2013

The division that I managed at Washington Mutual included at various times a research, architecture and planning group complete with a business intelligence team, application and technology architects, and a technology recovery team; an office of business continuity; an office of regulatory and audit assurance for the technology group; a technology change management group; and both application and vendor information security groups. All these groups provide regular reports to executives and, in some cases, to the board of directors.

I believe I hold the record for reshaping technical analysis and recommendations into executive summaries. If the summaries do not clearly make the case, they will not be funded, particularly these days when executives have access to cable television and other media who showcase experts on topics like cybersecurity breaches or mitigation plans for the nation's crumbling infrastructure. Several decisions by the Federal Trade Commission of late, notably the Wyndham Hotel case, have underscored the responsibility of the board in the area of cybersecurity. This article explains to risk and security experts how their reports can have real impact and free up the necessary budget.

The identification of operational risk exposure does not mean that it is easy to mitigate the risk. Often closure depends upon additional funds, and that means a proposal must be made to executives. In the best of all possible worlds, the funds are obtained because of the clarity of the request; and the executive team has also understood better the risk around the exposure. Often, however, the funds are not forthcoming because the request is not understood or because the priority for funding is not established. From our work, we have learned how to make the pitch into the executive suite, and we wish to share some of the rudimentary practices that will sharpen your own pitch.

Earlier in my career, I was a grant writer. I loved the symmetry involved in making the case – creating a beginning, middle and end to the argument on why my institution deserved the grant and for what purpose we would use the funds. Because usually there was a cover sheet on a grant proposal that required an abstract, high level summary of the request, I grew adept at summarizing worthiness and urgency. In the business world, we call the cover page of such a request for funds the "executive summary" and I have provided in Figure 1 an outline of the key points to be covered in an executive summary.

Whether it's funding to improve your company's fraud program, or to enhance your information security or business continuity programs, or even funds to respond to the latest piece of regulation to descend upon your institution, a thoughtful, strategic approach has the best results.

Consider the life of the CEO. Financial risk is always present. There's a board of directors to be managed. New regulations continue to appear, especially in the banking and health- care sectors, at least in the U.S. Reputational risk damage lurks in blind spots. And most meetings that a CEO conducts with his own team involve a briefing with unpleasant information or a request for more budget. How do you break through the noise to make your case?

1. Your own staff will have prepared an exhaustive technical analysis on the gap you are trying to close. Edit that analysis to remove overly-technical terms or acronyms. Then attach this longer analysis behind your executive summary. Make sure that you have several non-experts read the full document before you present it to the CEO, to ensure that what you are saying and how you are saying it can be understood.

2. Assume in writing your executive summary that the CEO will not read the whole document. Your case must be made in the executive summary. All the rest is additional justification for the request itself.

3. Pay close attention to your writing style. As one who both writes and edits, I would say that your greatest challenge is in

the tone. You don't want to cry wolf, but neither do you want to underestimate the complexity of the risk exposure. Say clearly what could happen if the gap is not fixed and be sure to provide both a minimum fix option as well as a description with costs of the optimum solution. Your tone should also reflect calm command of the problem being presented by the gap, and confidence that you have outlined minimum and optimum solutions. To do all this while speaking plain English may be a challenge, but it is one to take seriously. If you look at the challenges facing companies right now, for example from cyber-intruders, and look at the amount of media coverage that ranges from in-depth to inaccurate on this topic, then you see that your job is first to provide accurate background information on the problem for your industry, and then to state clearly how the problem affects your particular institution. If on the other hand, you are seeking funds based upon lessons learned from a recent event, say fines paid on Libor price fixing, then you will spend less time on describing the conditions that led to the fine than you do on what types of risk exposure your particular institution is facing if controls are not reexamined within your company.

4. Read great orators for an above-average command of language. You'll gain a better sense of what it means to persuade. Two of my favorite orators to re-read are Abraham Lincoln and Winston Churchill, both of whom wrote and spoke during times of war.

5. Write your executive summary so that it could be sent on by the CEO to the board of directors or to the regulators if extraordinary funds or risk exposure are at the heart of your summary.

6. End the document ahead of your meeting with the CEO so she/he has time to read it before you meet. Listen carefully to the questions you get in the meeting, and use them to better tailor your next request.

Above all, remember that the request is not about you, but rather about the operational risk exposure or gap you are trying to reduce.

Every Wall is a Door
Issue 18, June 2013

I wrote this article early on in my current profession as a teacher. Though I had created internship programs for college students at institutions as different as the Seattle Art Museum or Delphi Computers & Peripherals, sustained teaching in a formal classroom context is a different matter. I would hope that this article illuminates the joy of teaching as well as some of the questions that my students continue to ask about the practice of risk management.

My approach to teaching is both committed and practical, preparing professional students to become next generation leaders in the practice of risk management. Each of the courses I teach has its own rhythms and variations and has been tweaked each time I teach it as appropriate. As a teacher I have learned that each quarter, each student, and each group of students, has a different set of challenges from which to approach the work, and I do my best to see to it that the structure and content of my courses remains open to change. I encourage students to provide direct comments on the courses I teach during the quarter; but also use the student evaluations from the end of the quarter to tell me what works and what doesn't. I use those comments as a basis to rework my courses quarter by quarter. I believe that teachers best serve their students by listening to their input and staying responsive to their insights. Real learning is always a two-way street.

Those students interested in risk-related careers – and I include those here who will take jobs in cyber-security and compliance – have never had so many opportunities for employment. The world has become a more dangerous place. In 2017 it was estimated that there are over one million unfilled cybersecurity positions, and that the number would grow to 3.5 million jobs by 2021. The ability to perform risk-related assessments and to analyze machine learning data is already highly valued, and the need for specialists who can think outside the box and incorporate risk-related questions into their assessments will only become more valuable.

I started teaching about operational risk at the University of Washington's Information School a little more than a year ago. I've designed two courses for graduate students on operational risk that are now permanent parts of the curriculum. Answering questions from graduate students keeps me intellectually nimble. The students have no stake in the questions except their own curiosity. As I answer, new patterns and sometimes themes start to emerge from the material on which we are focused. And there you have it: answering to students in a seminar is quite different than preparing consultant reports or making a presentation to respectful executives, where both culture and the politics of an institution must be taken into account.

In a perfect world, we could each think, teach, and write at some scale about what we understand of operational risk. For me, the desire is strong to change the way we think about the subject; to influence the next generation of operational risk practitioners; and to build a heightened awareness of risk tolerances in those on the business side, as well as in those who will manage our security, business continuity, audit and regulatory programs of the future.

One of the first things a teacher does is to create a course syllabus that includes textbook(s) and readings. Finding good textbooks for either course is a challenge. Though there are a number of books with the words "operational risk management" or "enterprise risk management" or "COSO" in the title, most of these books are dry as dust, often written by auditors. Since both courses also track real world operational risk issues, it is understood that additional reading and discussion from current events is required. In this quarter, looking at both the public and private sector in the advanced risk course, we've not been short of examples across multiple sectors: governance questions at JPMorgan Chase, the US Internal Revenue Service, the US Justice Department, and the US Department of Homeland Security; cyber challenges from Chinese and Iranian hackers; disasters in Bangladesh and Oklahoma; privacy risk from new technology such as Google Glass or various kinds of wearable clothing;

emerging public health threats from both the Asian H7N9 virus and the Saudi norovirus; and terrorism at the Boston Marathon and in London. From this list, you can deduce that we examine risk primarily in six critical infrastructure sectors – banking and finance, energy, information technology, communications, public health and emergency services.

Here are some of the questions that students have asked in the past year, and that you yourself may have been asking, as an operational risk manager:

Is this a young field?
Yes, it's early days yet, to my mind. I once heard a market risk expert describe operational risk as everything that is not market or credit risk. I prefer the Basel definition that looks through the lens of people, process, systems, and external events. Though we have increasingly sophisticated COSO and Basel frameworks and increasing layers of regulation, especially in the financial sector, we have yet to prove our usefulness to executives making business-based decisions.

Even if I learn how to recognise and quantify the risk, who will listen to me in a corporate setting?
And therein the rub: How to distinguish operational risk managers from compliance or from internal audit personnel? I am on my second textbook where equivocation and dithering takes place about where operational risk should report. My own view is that operational risk should build its programs in a federated manner, from the ground up, so that "first responders" are actually in the line of business rather than in an oversight function. So part of the answer here depends upon being able to say how operational risk is a value add-on rather than an overhead burden. Since most business people do not believe that those in risk, compliance or audit functions actually understand the business from the inside out, taking the time to do so could mean all the difference. Sitting with the business as it is, maps its strategic planning and allows risk assessment to be grounded in the "what if?" premise, rather than seen as either a "yes man" or as a predictable "too dangerous" response. In fact, we want business to take risks, but with consideration of what could go wrong, and what type of agile response it would take to self-correct

downstream. This is where good risk management, operational or market or credit, begins: with the business. I wrote several months ago (Perfect Pitch, *The Risk Universe*, March 2013) about how to frame up emerging risk projects in the form of executive briefings.

Aren't some levels of loss acceptable if the end is still accomplished?
It depends upon the risk appetite established at the highest level of the company. A good example would be the London Whale loss at JPMorgan Chase. The company is enormously profitable, and though the loss of more than $6 billion may look large to us, it was considered small from the perspective of the overall investment portfolio designed to offset losses elsewhere. The bank appears to be mired in two indirectly-related issues that are part of an operational risk pattern: a lack of succession planning and increased regulatory scrutiny as well. There is no doubt that the bank's reputation, as well as that of its CEO, was impacted. But shareholders just reconfirmed their confidence in both the CEO and the governance structure in the 2013 annual meeting. There seems to be no doubt that the board level risk committee will be strengthened. It remains to be seen if the internal risk management function can be federated at JPMC, so it begins with first responders in the lines of business. Shifts in culture are not unlike turning very large ships in small channels.

Why should there be an expectation that employees behave any better than their bosses?
This is the perennial question. Though all of our leadership courses teach that tone is set at the top of the corporation, we have proliferating examples of non- executives like Sherron Watkins at Enron, who shine a light upon fraud, corruption or malfeasance. We design our training courses around ethics for employees, not for executives. We don't easily reward candour in the board room or the executive suite if it is going to affect growth or profits. Of course, we don't always reward managers for notifying us about risks either.

That's why I am a teacher at this point: to affect change all the way through the corporation, including at the executive level. To understand the facts of a risk clearly, to analyze what the costs of inaction will be before a decision is made one way or the other, is not yet an executive habit. But it could be. At a time when we are facing so many threats from so many different operational risk situations around the globe, this is a place to begin. As Ralph Waldo Emerson said, "Every wall is a door."

Remembering 9/11
Issue 21, September 2013

I wrote this article for a mostly British audience twelve years after the World Trade Center towers, a portion of the Pentagon, and nearly 3,000 people were annihilated. No one ever forgets where they were on the morning of September 11, 2011, and that's what this article is about – lessons learned in Seattle that led to improved crisis management across all critical infrastructure sectors. The lessons that we take away from the day in addition to the improved disaster response measures that I discuss in this article are various. The response from the government was overwhelmingly militaristic: 22 different government agencies were pulled into a new cabinet department, and named "Homeland Security." The defense and state departments crafted a military strike plan to retaliate in several Middle Eastern countries. Ordinary Muslim citizens were spit upon, and in New York City approval to build a new mosque near the World Trade Center was withheld. In responding to the tragic loss of life and property, we can see now how the government overreacted and, in doing so, set in motion a current state of affairs in 2018 where we are suspicious of those who look different than us, who speak another language, and who dress in alignment with their religious or cultural values.

Historians have their work cut out for them in understanding whether assimilation or multiculturalism is the best course where immigrants are concerned, especially after 9/11. Sunni Islamist multi-national religious fervor drove the 19 Al-Qaeda hijackers to destroy the twin towers, the symbolic center of infidel banking and to try to destroy two other American symbols, the Pentagon and the White House. In this article, I begin with the 7/7/7 London subway bombings, the first instance where we began to wonder why second generation Muslims who appeared to be assimilated into British culture would carry out such a terrible set of actions, and be willing to die performing them. I mention the 1995 Oklahoma City federal courthouse bombing as the closest equivalent before 9/11 in the United States, carried out by two aggrieved white nationalists who saw government as the enemy and the bombing itself as payback for two earlier incursions by federal law enforcement at Ruby Ridge and Waco. Today violent white nationalists groups bear a remarkable resemblance to Al-Qaeda in the intensity of their hatred and their commitment to increasingly sophisticated forms of violence.

The current Trump administration has enabled such groups, inflaming elements in our society who are already afraid of Muslims, Hispanics and people of color. Its immigration policies specifically preclude citizens of certain Mideast countries from entering this country, and billions of dollars are being spent on border security. Ironically, many of the measures meant to reassure Americans after 9/11 about their personal safety have led to heightened resentments and paranoia. At this time, it is unclear how much havoc one administration can wreak on constitutional principles and our way of life.

The 2005 London subway bombings carried out at multiple locations are embedded in the memories of British first responders, operational risk experts and ordinary people, including those who can recall the London Blitz of 1940-41. For the first time at a widespread level, survivors photographed themselves and used social media for updates to say they were alive. Some of us in the United States studied those bombings for what they could tell us on home-grown terrorism and militant Islam. For Americans, who had really not experienced any form of domestic terrorism since the 1995 Oklahoma City federal courthouse bombing, we have an imprecise but equally harrowing equivalent: the three locations in the United States that were hit by planes taken over by terrorists on 9/11. The operational risk challenges in identifying terrorism in both countries are very high to this day.

On that day, having listened to an early radio broadcast that the Manhattan towers had been hit by airplanes, I drove to work at Washington Mutual Bank because I had a team to lead. I listened to additional details as I looked about in driving in. Was Seattle at risk? I was not at that time a member of the bank's crisis management team, but I was responsible for over 100 people, who looked to me for direction. I can honestly say that most of my expertise as a crisis manager was learned at high cost that day.

People: Executives of the bank were holed up in a makeshift command center, watching a single television set. There were no communications out, either to managers or to employees. Even though there were two tiers of executives who could have communicated – the executive committee or the crisis management team – we were on our own. In retrospect, I believe that executives were trying to gather sufficient information to send out a communication but ended up too horrified and paralysed to act.

Process: There had been little or no formal process for recovery from the 6.8 magnitude Nisqually earthquake in Seattle earlier in 2001. And there was none now. Everything was done by the seat of the pants outside the data center, which appeared to be operating just fine. I spent several hours trying to find the answer to "Shall we dismiss our people or ask them to work?" I could find nothing in the bank's policies or my orientation manual that would give me direction. Once a fellow manager explained the concept of "manager discretion," I told my team that they would be paid that day whether they chose to stay at work or to go home. I eventually walked across the street to the makeshift command center, knocked on the door and asked to speak to the CIO, who agreed that communications to employees were important and promised to get on it. On this day, the crisis management team was not heard from. My comments about that team can be found here in the operational risk category of "external events".

Systems: The Washington Mutual network was up, both the internet and the intranet platforms, but it was not being utilised effectively. We had employees on the East Coast, several in fact based or expected to be in meetings on the World Trade Center 16-acre campus, but it took a long time to locate them because most lines had been knocked out in Manhattan. In those days, SMS messaging was not so common.

External Events: The bank had a crisis management team with roughly 23 senior managers as members that would be activated in the event of any major disaster. Crisis management in those days consisted of long conference calls, often scheduled at the same time the lines of business were running their own calls. In theory, information would flow from the lines of business to the crisis management team so that communications could flow to employees. After 9/11, the technology group was asked to appoint two members to the team, and I volunteered along with my colleague, the head of technology infrastructure. We spent several years as committee members trying to winnow down the team and push for more definition – and shorter calls. When eventually, I was asked to take over continuity of operations for Washington Mutual in 2003, I became chair of the crisis management team and reduced the team size from 25 to 8. We never activated the crisis management team unless the line(s) of business asked for help. We increased the number of annual scenario tests from two to 12. Our approach became a federated one to disaster response.

The crisis management team was there to help make decisions that were larger than any single line of business: "Determining whether employees should stay at work, report to work or work from home; Evacuating employees if necessary from foreign locations; Determining whether emergency assistance may be offered to employees; Authorising unusual expenses... such [as] ...extra security personnel to monitor a facility that has been damaged; Authorising internal and external communications; Consideration then action on legal advice that may cover a wide range of topics, from liability to reputational risk exposure; Updates to regulators and to boards of directors, so that there are no surprises."

Some things have changed in that approach over the past five years as I work with various companies to streamline their people, process, systems and respond to external events. Because of near-immediate, real-time coverage of events, hierarchies collapse between reporting teams, especially in the area of cyber response, where incident response teams become the crisis response. Emergency management protocols around anticipating large storms like Hurricane Sandy have been refined and simplified so that there can be both local and governmental responses that work in synch with one another.

In this country, we have never lost so many first responders on one day. The communications failures that day, especially those where police and firefighters were unable to talk to each other by radio, loom large still and are documented in the 9/11 Commission Report. The commission recommended a national interoperable broadband communications network for emergency first responders to communicate with one another. Twelve years after 9/11, we are not any further along in this effort because it requires Congressional legislation and approval. We have only to look at large scale events like Hurricane Sandy to see how beneficial such a dedicated radio spectrum would be. Imagine even more: than the private sector would be allowed to listen on the same spectrum so as to have immediate access to decisions as they were made.

There is more than enough work still to do, for all of us, not just the Congress. The world has sped up and decisions need to be announced soon after CNN or the BBC starts covering a disaster. To get a firm handle on operational risk management, we have been recommending increased and varied scenario testing, and the creation of "canned" messaging for various types of events that can be deployed within minutes. Given the discipline behind such testing and tiered messages, it becomes possible also for companies to measure just how much financial loss they might suffer from each type of event.

Vendor risk and intellectual property
Issue 23, November 2013

Though we are seeing novel uses of existing copyright law with movements like open source and copyleft, most intellectual property – including copyrights, patents, trademarks and trade secrets – is still closely guarded and defended in both the public and private sector. We are probably most familiar with the ongoing infringement lawsuits between Apple and Samsung, or between Disney and an infringer, but every company, especially those who do business globally, worries increasingly about theft of secrets that could be commoditized in another country to compete at a lower price against its own products. A variant of that concern is the publication by Shadow Brokers, a hacker group that first appeared in 2016, of classified secrets stolen from the National Security Agency and released for sale on the public market, at least one of which was responsible for the ransomware exploit called WannaCry.

Unmitigated operational risk exists where vendors are contracted without the appropriate safeguards in place. Here I discuss Edward Snowden's role as a Booz Allen contractor with access to National Security Administration highly classified documents that he was able to remove and arrange to publicize. Snowden claims to have tried to discuss his concerns about the material with his supervisor. Though government officials thought he should have used the U.S. Whistleblower Act, that act does not cover contractors, only full time employees. Then too, the government's manner of over-classifying documents differs from designations in the private sector, generally including "for internal use only" or "confidential" or "restricted."

A more recent data breach involves a third party vendor doing background checks and the U.S. Office of Personnel Management, where a data breach occurred that includes documentation around all those seeking a security clearance. The material lost is an extremely valuable form of intellectual property, believed to being held for an elaborate future exploit by a nation state seeking to impersonate and understand the privileges of those who hold top secret clearance.

British and American operational risk experts have had a lot to absorb since Edward Snowden started releasing documents he filched during his time as a Booz Allen contractor at the National Security Agency (NSA). There may very well be a handful of NSA executives who have a good idea of just how much material will eventually be published by the media, but I think most of us (including the Obama administration) are surprised at the range and variety of the materials about British and American projects involving targeted surveillance. Just when we think we have seen the last set of materials, more appear. In succession, we have been able to read about programs such as Prism, Boundless Informant, XKeyscore, and Tempora -- as well as documents that expose how successful the NSA has been at latching on to data from both Google and Yahoo through penetration of its secure links among global data centers.

Many of us had been aware of the government's heavy reliance upon contractors to do its work, especially since threat analysis was ratcheted up after 9/11. Like the government, we just assumed that companies like Booz Allen did a good job of vetting the persons they hired to work on classified information. Recently we learned that it was not only Booz Allen's background checks that were deficient. In 2009, while Snowden was working for the CIA "his supervisor wrote a derogatory report in his personnel file, noting a distinct change in the young man's behavior and work habits, as well as a troubling suspicion."[*New York Times*, October 11, 2013].The supervisor's suspicion was that he was trying to break into classified files. Evidently that information stayed buried in his personnel file or "fell through the cracks," and was not picked up on a subsequent background check for his more recent position as a contractor at Booz Allen.

Operational risk that stems from vendors and their contractors is, in fact, one of the most critical risks that business faces in an increasingly complex world. The US government may be the largest entity to contract with vendors, but the practice of using contractors permeates most mid-sized and large companies. Gaps in vendor controls can be found in any of the four lenses through which we view operational risk – people, broken or failed processes, systems, and external events.

In a March 2012 Impact Factor study, more than 100 companies were surveyed on their use of supply chains. The results were not encouraging. Half of those surveyed spent $50,000 or less annually to audit and assess suppliers. And 80% of those surveyed indicated they manage only the primary vendor, not what are often multiple layers of suppliers and subcontractors. With increased outsourcing and offshoring over the past five years, the stakes have never been higher. Economic turmoil, more natural disasters and political change around the globe have produced additional complexity for vendors and for their clients.

As companies grow, their intellectual property is often not well protected. In a Carnegie Mellon CERT study on such threats, contractors were the heart of the problem: in one case, a contract janitor stole customer account information from hard copy documents lying out on desks and used it to obtain credit cards in the customers' names (loss = over $200,000); and in another case, a contractor stole and sold trade secret drawings intended for shredding (loss = $100 million). For more information on Carnegie Mellon's CERT research, go to http://www.cert.org/insider_threat/. Though we don't have a great deal of detail on how contractor Edward Snowden obtained access above his own level to so many documents, one can infer that the NSA has now tightened up its access controls as well as its internal logging routines.

The first place to start in managing the risk around vendors and intellectual property is with the contract that is created. Here's specific advice by operational lens:

People: Require background checks scaled in sophistication to the criticality of the business processes you are giving the vendor. Identify whether the vendor is using subcontractors and require background checks there if appropriate. Be mindful also of the small companies you need to run your business, like janitors or couriers.

Process: Bind the vendor on all compliance-related issues (in particular, their own business continuity and data security programs and those of their subcontractors). Ask them to show you their plans for how they will service your account in the event of events like natural disasters, pandemics, or acts of terrorism in this or other countries. Write into the contract the time frame in which you expect the vendor's attention during such events. Above all, trap for potential worst case scenarios and for additional layers of subcontractors.

Systems: Require proof of additional layers of redundancy that the vendor has in place. Consider geopolitical location if data centers are involved. Insist upon site inspection visits to critical vendors. Before you contract a cloud vendor, determine in advance how you will audit that vendor and write it into the contract.

External Events: Closely review the vendor's business continuity and security plans. Find critical gaps in both your own and your vendor's plans based on increased global complexity for transactions processing.

Vendor risk management has two parts: getting the contract language right; and active monitoring of critical vendors. The commonest problem I see is that small vendors are not scrutinized in the same way that large technology vendors are, even though small vendors often have direct access to intellectual property.
Finally, build your own corporate assumptions on service and recovery into each contract: what priority will your company have with a cash courier, for example, during a severe weather event? Once you've worked out all those details and embedded the understanding in the contract, then insist upon key vendor participation in the scenario testing you do throughout the year. And keep your board of directors apprised several times a year on the controls you have in place to avert financial loss or reputational damage.

Are living wills the answer?
Issue 26, February 2014

From the Federal Reserve Board Bulletin: "Section 165(d) of the Dodd-Frank Wall Street Reform and Consumer Protection Act requires that bank holding companies with total consolidated assets of $50 billion or more and nonbank financial companies designated by the Financial Stability Oversight Council (FSOC) for supervision by the Federal Reserve periodically submit resolution plans to the Federal Reserve and the Federal Deposit Insurance Corporation. Each plan, commonly known as a living will, must describe the company's strategy for rapid and orderly resolution in the event of material financial distress or failure of the company, and include both public and confidential sections. Currently, the largest, most complex banking organizations supervised by the Board are required to file resolution plans by July 1 of each year. All other companies supervised by the Board and subject to the resolution planning rule generally are required to file by December 31 of each year."

Some years later, how are the eight big banks doing? Reuters reported in 2017 that the Federal Reserve and Federal Deposit Insurance Corporation found "shortcomings in plans from Bank of America, Goldman Sachs, Morgan Stanley and Wells Fargo, detailing how they could be safely taken apart should they face bankruptcy. Regulators found no problems with plans submitted by Bank of New York Mellon, Citigroup, J.P. Morgan Chase, or State Street."

The Trump administration has already begun to unwind the Dodd-Frank Act. At the time of this writing, Congress is voting to relax the Dodd-Frank rules for small and midsize banks, raising the threshold for tighter oversight from $50 billion to $250 billion in assets and carving out small mortgage lenders from new reporting around racial and income data around loans. Nothing in the legislation ties the hands of regulators if they observe risky *behavior. Next up in the sights of the administration: the Volcker Rule, which restricts all banks from making certain kinds of investments that do not benefit their customers by using customers' money to make proprietary (and often high risk) trades.*

The first and second waves of "living will" compliance for banks and depository institutions with consolidated assets of more than $50 billion has elicited a fair amount of scepticism with a few dashes of scorn. Because of the liability around preparing such documents for the regulators in aid of the Dodd-Frank Act (DFA) Rule and the Insured Depository Institution Rule (DI Rule), the documents are generally prepared by lawyers rather than business leaders or the board of directors of an institution. It's not just American banks that must comply: foreign banks that have US branches as well as any nonbank financial company designated as "a systematically significant financial institution (SSFI)" must also submit a living will.

In your personal life, creating such a document is relatively easy if you are a thoughtful person: you identify the person who can make medical decisions for you if you are incapacitated; and you specify with the some degree of clarity just what measures you wish taken to keep you alive under certain conditions. The intent behind the DFA/DI rulemaking is that the measures to be taken will not keep you alive. Rather, they will save the regulators and the courts the burden of figuring out where to sell off the assets to avert any cost to the financial system or its taxpayers. That is the assumption, at least. From FDIC Board minutes in September of 2011, we see that there is a determination by the FDIC to get out from under funding critical operations during such a resolution process, and "to facilitate improved efficiencies and risk management practices amongst systemically important financial institutions as they produce and evaluate these plans." For a financial institution, however, to specify where its assets might be sold expeditiously is only a small part of what is required by the DFI and DI Rules. A bank's living will must take into account insolvency law, change of control provisions, tax and corporate law. This is good news for law firms who will end up preparing such documents. "They are an exercise while things are fine, prepared by lawyers and not representative of what might happen," said Mark Williams, a former Federal Reserve

bank examiner and a professor of finance at Boston University."
[*New York Times*, July 3, 2012]

Creation of the living wills is an expensive proposition, an outgrowth of the 2008 financial collapse. They satisfy a regulatory requirement that is unlikely to change over the next decade. But will preparing these living wills be sufficient to avert losses that seem inevitable as a result of the interconnectedness of such large and complex institutions? Given that the living will will be with us for some years, what could banks be doing internally to ensure the viability of their institutions the next time we experience such a downturn – that is, to survive rather than to be taken apart?

I cut my operational risk teeth in the field of business continuity planning, in which most scenarios imagined posit significant financial loss during short-term setbacks like data center outages, hacked websites, hurricanes, wildfires, floods, tornadoes or earthquakes. The question that is asked first of any critical business process is: "What if it was not available for one hour/two hours/four hours/eight hours/24 hours/48 hours? How long could you live without it?" In order to answer that question, one has to trace the interdependencies between a critical business process, its technology platform(s) and third party vendors, and its relationship to other business being done by the institution. Answers to these questions and others that are part of a Business Impact Analysis (BIA) represent for me the foundation of an operational risk framework, particularly when one includes the scenario tests that are a part of a world class continuity planning program.

In answering the key questions to produce a living will, the lawyers will almost certainly reference an institution's business continuity plan, often the only inventory of its core business lines and critical operations and functions. It seems likely that existing contingency planning programs will evolve to stay in synch with the living will document and should begin to test broader economic scenarios that are already a part of the Basel program. Other than the living will and business contingency planning programs, where else might executives and regulators look to shore up the resiliency of an institution?

I recommend that both boards of directors and regulators look closely at the strength of an executive succession planning program. While implemented well at middle and senior management levels in many banks, it appears to be unsuccessful or nonexistent at executive levels. It is still a very delicate matter for boards of directors to insist that a Chief Executive Officer identify and develop potential successors. The banking and insurance industry is known for nearly Shakespearean twists and turns in this area. Tracing a single example might look like this: Jamie Dimon was at one time the heir apparent to Sanford Weil at Citigroup. When he left Citigroup, he went on to make a larger and more complex bank from the merger of Bank One and JPMorgan. Over the years, JPMorgan Chase has had any number of senior executive understood to be on the "successor track" but who have given up and left the bank. Dimon is sitting in the catbird seat still: he enjoys the dual titles of chairman and CEO still. Before the last annual board meeting, the media reported that he told the board he would leave the bank if the chairman title were removed; and that appeared to be sufficient warning for large investors to vote that he retain both titles. Does the "living will" requirement take situations such as this into account? Who will compel Dimon to put a genuine succession program into action? Looking past JPMorgan Chase to other large banks, how many have succession plans in place against scenarios that include a CEO dying, or perhaps injured and out of the office for up to six months?

Both contingency planning and succession planning can be considered as tools to enhance living wills. Rather than focus on winding down a large and complex institution, they offer forward looking and practical opportunities for sustained growth and profitability.

Starting with the Lehman Brothers failure on September 15, 2008, a total of $16.7 billion in deposits was removed over a ten day period from Washington Mutual, which led to the FDIC seizure and sale to JPMorgan Chase. That seizure cost depositors nothing because of the way the FDIC structured the deal. Would a living will or a scenario test have saved the bank? I have my doubts. The seizure happened without advance warning. The bank lacked an internal successor to the former Chairman/CEO, and was rife with misplaced confidence from the board that it was making its case effectively in Washington DC. Not even a living will plan would have been sufficient to dampen the view that things were turning around, that there was no need to pull the plug. In short, a living will is no substitute for hubris. Can we honestly say that would not still be the case if a large bank ran into rather similar trouble today?

Insider threats escalate operational risk
Issue 30, June 2014

In 2016, I published a whole chapter on the three major root causes of conduct risk. I identified them as tone at the top, culture and conflicts of interest. Insider threats are part of conduct risk and can range from providing inappropriate access to confidential data, to selling trade secrets, to insider trading, or to the internal falsification of group accounting reports in order to preserve bonuses. It is hard to overestimate the impact of the group upon the decisions that the group leader makes. An illustration might be rogue trader Nick Leeson, who brought down Barings Bank by making "increasingly outsize bets to try to get back to the profit side of the books over three years." (Searle, Conduct Risk: A Practitioner's Guide, *p.43). He described that period of time as not wanting to let his team down. So too did Toshihide Iguchi have similar motives in his rogue trading with Daiwa Bank, describing it as personal dishonor to let down other members of his team. At Wells Fargo, what we thought was behavior contained in the community banking area now appears to be more widespread with recent news of the alteration of client banking documents in the business division in the areas of auto loans and mortgage interest rates. Evidently the organizational changes that have already been made are insufficient to the challenge.*

When will firms start taking insider threats seriously? Does something have to go very wrong before a mechanism is set up to better understand outlier behavior? What kinds of tools have we developed for identifying the outliers before matters spin out of control?

As a CEO, you want to believe your company excels at retaining the best and brightest employees and that your employees behave at all times with integrity. Yet there are enough examples to make you think more about the problems that your employees and contractors can cause – not surprising, since employees and contractors represent your largest risk, with a median loss of $140,000 per event for insider fraud (employee theft, fraud or embezzlement) and an average $20,000 in damage to the company from other insider attacks (data leaks, intellectual property theft, etc). This data comes from the 2012 Association of Certified Fraud Examiners (ACFE) Report to the Nation. Add this to the 2013 Identity Theft Resource Center Report and you will have a very clear picture of the frequency and the financial costs of various types of insider threats.

Since 2001, the Carnegie Mellon CERT (www.cert.org) has been engaged in research on insider threats and, since 2004, CERT has produced annual reports on such threats in partnership with the US Secret Service. From those reports, which can be found on the CERT website, it is possible to paint a useful picture of the ways in which a corporate culture could be at risk for heightened insider threats and to develop a checklist of behaviours that might cause management or HR departments to take additional precautions against, when appropriate.

Most executives would agree that an organisation's most valuable assets are its people and its intellectual property. Accordingly, the primary defence should be time spent training employees on insider threats. Enlightened employees become long-term employees when their orientation and training includes understanding what an organisation values, how it is protected and who owns it.

In her presentation to the 2012 BAI conference "Outing Insider Fraud," Shirley Inscoe noted that leaking bank information is the most pervasive form of financial insider fraud and identified additional types as "falsifying loan documents, selling bank or customer information, misuse of assets or position, taking money from cash drawers, identity theft and mortgage theft."

But there are more types of insider threats than financial fraud. Dawn Capelli, who at the time headed this work at the Carnegie Mellon CERT, spoke some years ago at a Shared Assessments Summit organized by The Santa Fe Group, where she summarised aspects of their work as the CERT's "Common Sense Guide on Insider Threats." This made me wonder if understanding and sharing some of the reasons that employees engage in this behaviour might facilitate managers more proactively looking for early warning signs. In the context primarily of workplace violence, I referenced some of these behaviours that managers can look for in the third chapter of my book, *Advice From A Risk Detective.*

There is no doubt that putting controls in place to prevent different types of insider threats can reduce or eliminate financial or reputational loss, though it is a much more complex effort than it would have been even five years ago. Employees have a great deal of physical and electronic access by virtue of their status, as do contractors working as critical business partners. As CERT points out, both employees and contractors have practical understanding of how well or poorly policies and controls are managed. So let's explore some examples of the high level behaviours to look out for.

Anger and aggrievement: Capelli described situations in which very smart developers came to see the applications they were working on as belonging to them because they had created them, rather than the company. When circumstances deteriorate, the developer can cause damage to the application or share its code with outsiders.

Shame: A number of traders fall into this category when they feel shame for incurring large losses, which they then hide and then gamble further to correct the losses by continuing to trade larger amounts outside organisational controls. The JPMorgan Chase London Whale episode is an example of compounding losses.

Poor performance reviews: Capelli's team worked with the Secret Service and interviewed a number of former employees now serving jail time for their insider crimes. A pretty consistent theme is that the former employee had almost always been highly valued in previous performance reviews, but then received a poor review, leading to feelings of anger and aggrievement, which led to theft.

Anxiety from organisational change: When a company is being sold, anxiety that an employee will lose his/her job can cause him/ her to inappropriately remove corporate information for personal use or other nefarious purposes.

In addition to providing solid orientation and training to employees and training managers to spot troubling behaviours, what else can be done? Background checks on potential hires would be the first place to start looking for flags. When interviewing potential employees, hiring managers should be checking not only for the answers they wish to hear, but also for culture fit with the firm. In high risk positions that include broad administrative-level access, a probationary period is certainly appropriate, with additional follow-up meetings between management and the new employee to ensure that the new employee has a growing understanding of the workplace. If we take Edward Snowden's actions as an example, where we are looking at a large corporation with sensitive electronic property, I would recommend that employees with privileged access to both internal servers and other documents on outside servers be subject to the "two-man rule", which requires at least two people to approve an action in order for it to take place. The NSA announced the implementation of this rule only after thousands of files had walked out the virtual door with Snowden. The General Motors legal and safety divisions provide us with yet another example.

We see two groups that grew to become enormous insider threats, not because they divulged confidential information, but rather because they methodically concealed negative information from their superiors. This behaviour, which has been described alternately as "overly bureaucratic" or "criminal," identifies the insider threat of the elimination or concealment of information known to be problematic or expensive to the firm. Frankly, we don't know how often suppression or concealment of information occurs in large companies – but I will be looking into this type of threat in my next book, *Executives and Risk: What Your Teams Won't Tell You*. More to come.

Ebola risk — from epidemic to pandemic?
Issue 33, September 2014

As I write this headnote in May of 2018, we have just been informed of the departure of the head of global health security on the National Security Council just a day after an Ebola outbreak was declared in the Democratic Republic of the Congo. The United States now has no single point person responsible for a U.S. response to ebola, or to health security, biodefense, and pandemic preparedness. These are not areas that the average American citizen thinks about on a regular basis, but the threat posed by a new ebola outbreak four years later in the continent of Africa is not good news. Indirectly related is the removal of the senior cybersecurity role in the government, by White House national security advisor John Bolton, who also eliminated the global health security role.

I first wrote about pandemics in 2007 for the British Journal of Business Continuity and Emergency Management, as the U.S. financial sector prepared using a scenario that imagined up to 40% of a firm's workforce could be affected for three months or more. Such a scenario involved creating a pandemic plan separate from a firm's all hazards business continuity plan, to understand which business processes could be suspended, which could be reduced, and which must continue at all costs. The financial sector also ran a full fledged pandemic test across the United States, not unlike the one conducted earlier in England, which produced a report with recommendations, especially around maintaining confidence in the financial system through an actual pandemic. At Washington Mutual, we had several opportunities to conduct our own pandemic tests with key vendors and first responders.

Today we must wonder about the availability of the ebola vaccine developed in 2015, and the role that the United States will play. Congress has provided funds for both global health security resources and for a cybersecurity role that spans all federal departments and agencies. Who will carry out the mission?

We have been watching the spread of Ebola in West Africa since spring. The stories are frightening to read. How can poor countries get in front of such an outbreak? What is their governments' role in communicating the types and sources of risk citizens are facing? Can they actually force citizens to drop cultural practices that span centuries? How is it that the World Health Organisation's budget is so reduced at such a time? Why is it that most of the alarm and pressure to take action has been raised by on-the-ground global organisations like Doctors Without Borders?

Seven years ago, it was a different matter when I first wrote on US financial sector planning for pandemic flu, specifically H5N1, for the British Journal of Business Continuity & Emergency Management (Volume 1, Number 3, March 2007).A year later, as the situation seemed to worsen, I wrote on additional pandemic planning steps taken by the US government and the banking and financial sector (Volume 2, Number 4, March 2008).A lot has changed in seven years. I believe that, based on the 2009 H1N1 pandemic flu campaign launched by the US Center for Diseases Control, we now understand that no plan to handle a public health crisis can be cast in concrete and issued with a user's manual, whether epidemic or pandemic.
If you're overseeing your firm's contingency plans, then are there practical steps you can take in anticipation of a virus that just may jump continents.

Review your critical business practices
Take a fresh look at your existing programme. What critical processes do you absolutely have to maintain in light of an assumed absentee rate of up to 40% at any given time? Which processes can you suspend during the event? Which processes can you performed less frequently, or on a reduced basis?

Who calls the shots?
This is literally one of the most challenging aspects of a worst case plan. You have to assume that your senior executives are just as vulnerable as your most valued front line or IT support employees. At Washington Mutual in 2006, we created a

"delegation of authority" form in which every executive and manager wrote down the names of 2-3 designees, in case he/she was out ill. We also identified the eight member crisis management team as the manager of the pandemic event, with each member having an alternate.

Clean up your employee contact information
Some organisations may have email addresses for employees, but no cell phone numbers. This precludes good use of text messaging during such an event. Obtaining a personal cell number may require that you explain and then explain again why you need it.

Travel Programme
Under what conditions will you ask an employee to travel to West Africa? Or through an airport that services West Africa? Do you have a programme that tracks locations of all employees flying on behalf of the company? What assistance would you provide to an employee who inadvertently was quarantined? If you don't now have such policies, you still have time to create them.

Check your vendors
Despite what's in the contract, how can your firm be sure you'll be made a priority during a pandemic, when your vendor will be equally disadvantaged as you are?

Check to be sure the vendor has a pandemic plan. We actually ended up writing it into our critical vendor contracts.

Map your infrastructure
Assume you can't do it all during a high impact event. "Identify customer-facing offices, administrative support facilities and ATM locations that will be kept open in main markets, and establish mechanisms to inform both customers and employees." [Searle, 2007] At Washington Mutual, we took a strategy developed during hurricanes in Florida and applied it across the country, setting criteria for the "hub branches" that would remain open, and communicate it in advance, so employees knew where to report and customers would know where they could get money.

Test Now
Once you have a plan, then begin testing it quarterly, sizing the impact of such an event up or down. This is how you continuously improve your plan; make it more flexible and applicable to situations outside public health crises. Holes still exist in most institutions' plan to have large numbers of employees telecommute. The assumption that the Internet would be available at a time when your children might be home from school playing games or watching movies is not well thought out.

Ah, the regulators!
Work now with regulators, country by country, to establish which business processes you normally use to communicate with them could be suspended or reduced during the event. Even the regulators will need to create plans around how they will continue to keep the cash moving.

These steps can be considered as good for your all-hazards plan as well as a pandemic plan. There are several specific steps you can take to better in case Ebola jumps continents.

Wash your hands often
As far as we know, Ebola is not currently an airborne virus. But it could mutate. But body fluids get attached to hands, which use door knobs, common utensils, office supplies, etc. Along with washing your hands frequently, try to keep your own workspace sanitized as well.

Get your flu vaccine
I remember reading a study that indicated that those who had a flu shot each year had built up a certain amount of possibly useful immunity against infectious diseases.

Pandemic payroll policies
Will you pay people some amount of their salary even if they are sick and/or have exceeded the number of sick days available? At Washington Mutual, we had determined to either extend everyone's amount of sick time by seven work days; or to pay them at the going disability rate. Ironically, the executives did not want employees to know that this would be the plan. Like so many other decisions, that was short- sighted. Had employees

known, they would have been informed and worked together to help cross train their fellow employees so that the institution would survive such an event.

All eyes are on the rapidly evolving situation in West Africa. The World Health Organisation is short of funds and supplies and personnel. Organisations like Doctors Without Borders are currently carrying the load. It is going to get much worse before it gets better, and it is going to take a long time to contain Ebola. First steps are underway now on trial vaccines or the use of Ebola survivors' blood. The cultural challenges are profound: what right do we have to tell them what to do? In the name of what? Nowhere have we ever seen the Digital Divide manifest itself so clearly as we are observing right now in West Africa. To those who say, "Don't worry, it won't affect us," I say tighten up your plans while you have time.

Dear member of the board
Issue 37, January 2015

Since 2015, we've witnessed more scandals from large companies with weak boards of directors. And regulators in this country and abroad have stepped in to underscore the role of a board member, not just to provide oversight of operations but also to weigh in against high risk ventures by firms. Two particular cases come to mind, both regulated by the Federal Trade Commission (FTC): in the first, a lawsuit alleged that "Target's board members and directors breached their fiduciary duties to the company by failing "to maintain proper internal controls" related to data security and misleading affected consumers about the scope of the breach after it occurred. " And in the second, that of the Wyndham Hotel data breach, "Under the terms of the settlement, the company will establish a comprehensive information security program designed to protect cardholder data – including payment card numbers, names and expiration dates. In addition, the company is required to conduct annual information security audits and maintain safeguards in connections to its franchisees' servers." (FTC website) The Wyndham board of directors was found to have failed in their fiduciary duties as well, and from that point forward firms have been on notice that their boards of directors must be kept informed often on the maturity of a given cybersecurity program. Regulators stepped in also with Wells Fargo, to insist upon the replacement of four board members along with hiring a new chief risk officer and what now totals more than one billion dollars of fines.

Though Uber is not yet a publicly traded company, its board of directors sought outside experts to examine the firm's culture and to determine whether or not its founding CEO should stay in place. In doing so, it exercised more of its fiduciary responsibilities than many publicly traded companies.

The advice in this article is meant to shore up timid board members, and show them that it is their job to look for trends or apparently unconnected pieces of information to mitigate risk in advance of a breach.

Whether you're a board member of a retailer like Starbucks or sitting on a large financial services board like JPMorgan Chase, I'll bet you're pleased at this point that you said no to Sony board membership. Though Enron is now nearly 13 years behind us, you may recall the US Senate subcommittee finding that ultimately led to the passage of the Sarbanes-Oxley (SOx) Act in 2002, that "the Enron Board of Directors failed to safeguard Enron shareholders and contributed to the collapse of the seventh largest public company in the United States, by allowing Enron to engage in high risk accounting, inappropriate conflict of interest transactions, extensive off-the- books activities, and excessive executive compensation."SOx better delineated the board's oversight role where financial accuracy is concerned, called for board level audit committees made up of outside (independent) directors, required attestation on internal controls, and emphasized that directors on boards are responsible for direct supervision of the company. At another level, it established independent oversight of public company audits, via the PCAOB (Public Company Accounting Oversight Board), fondly referred to as "peek-a-boo" to the profession, which had for the prior 100 years engaged in self- regulation. Over 2,000 firms from over 80 countries are registered with PCAOB today.

As financial losses mount from mismanaged vendors, gaps in internal controls and service outages from natural disasters or from cyber-attacks on publically- traded entities, many boards have paid more attention and modified selection criteria for its members. No longer are boards simply cheerleaders for the CEO. Technology has become more critical to high-speed digital transactions, so companies have sought out directors with IT chops, just like they have recruited independent experts to sit on their audit committees. But rarely do companies require significant continuing education for board members, especially on esoteric topics like strategic risk, high- speed trading, privacy, business continuity or cyber-threats. So it's entirely possible that a board member could read about the Target breach or the more recent Sony hack, ask a few questions and be reassured that it could not happen here.

If you're not already a member of (for example) the U.S. National Association of Corporate Directors (NACD), then how do you learn and what should you be looking for?

Overconfidence from the C-Suite
The belief that "it can't happen here" needs to be proved out to the board. If in fact, the board is not receiving threat or gap analyses directly from the Chief Information Security Officer and the Chief Internal Auditor on a quarterly basis, you should ask why not and raise the bar. For each explanation you receive from the executive team, you should ask how clearly the company's program is explained in terms of importance and relevance, to employees and customers, in a show of "tone at the top."

Vague or inaccurate responses to questions
Don't let executives "dumb down" explanations. Read widely in the company's lines of business, then be sure you get real answers to your questions. It is possible for executives to prepare briefing papers in clear English even though the material may be technical. In each case, the questions of risk and impact to revenues and reputation should be dealt with in addition to the costs being discussed.

Issues not on the radar
Sometimes the CEO and CFO do not have a clue as to what could be going wrong on the operational side. I'm looking closely at this issue in the book I'm working on right now. At each level of the company, analysis can get simplified in the name of "executive presentation" to the point that the CEO/CFO believes that the risk level is being managed, or is manageable. In such instances, it is not that the C-suite is trying to conceal information from the board, which is why one of your primary responsibilities as a board member is to ask questions based on information you've received from other sources or events experienced by other companies. A prime example here is General Motors, where damaging information and costs were concealed for years. Bad news or an unfavourable review of a new product/service always carries the potential for reduced support or loss of position, which is why no one likes to let his/her manager know when

sometime goes quite wrong. Asking questions is the best way to be sure that the board has all the information from a detailed briefing before making a decision.

Finally, look for the outliers
When you join a board, one of your first requests should be for the regulatory and audit reports over the past few years so that you can see where the gaps in controls are and to monitor what is being done to close the gaps. Are there consistent patterns, such as mis-handling of vendors or of confidential information? Is the technology up to date and redundant? What does the level of turnover look like at both the senior management and the executive level?

Well informed board members bring us one step closer to corporate stability.

ISIS is an operational risk
Issue 39, March 2015

Since 2014, I've researched and taught the so-called Islamic State (ISIS or ISIL) as an operational risk. Whether you examine it through the lens of information management ("ISIS does a great job) or of policy ("convert or die") or of ethics (recruiting videos, newsletters and a full range of paraphernalia), it's clear that ISIS has a five year plan to rule by restoring the boundaries of the Ottoman Empire. Despite the Trump administration's vow to eradicate ISIS, the group is still very much alive, though it has morphed over the years to play an outsize role in the training of lone wolves to wreak death and damage in their home countries. Some of these lone wolves never leave home for the training. ISIS operates both on the ground in the Mideast and online, via the training and promotional videos it makes available. Recently, Syria announced that ISIS has been driven out of Damascus, but we must ask ourselves for how long? At the same time, an Iraqi court sentenced the first group of over 1,000 "ISIS women" to death. The evolving situation with both Iran over the nuclear agreement; and in Iraq, where ISIS and Al-Qaeda still both operate on the ground; and in Syria, is volatile. From Martin Chulov and Nadia al-Faour for The Guardian on May 22, 2018: "More than 40,000 foreigners from 110 countries are estimated to have travelled to Iraq and Syria to join the jihadist group. Of those, around 1,900 are believed to have been French citizens, and around 800 were British."

London, Manchester and Paris seem to be the three European cities where ISIS delights in striking fear through massacre by truck or imploding explosive devices from one's bodies. In the United States, two of the most visible examples were the Orlando nightclub 2016 massacre as well as the San Bernardino 2015 shootings, both attributed to domestic terrorism inspired by online ISIS primers. Counter-terrorism specialists have stopped any number of other planned attacks before they happen, even as security has been tightened around public events where large numbers of people congregate.

A counter-terrorism official I heard speak several years ago likened Al-Qaeda as an organization to the Mafia, who has wider-reaching networks and longer term goals, as well as the strategic ability to carry out the events such as 9/11; and ISIS to street gangs who are much less strategic as they maintain a rough sort of discipline through the commission of horrific acts, here including subjugation, mass beheading of prisoners, idol-smashing, raping of women, all captured on high quality video for distribution on the internet.

Mitigation of this operational risk is not straightforward. The danger is that, as the poet William Blake noted, "you become what you behold."

Like you, I am deeply outraged at the increasingly horrific actions of the Islamic State of Iraq and the Levant (ISIS or ISIL), which in late June of 2014 rebranded itself to this designation, announced the formation of the Caliphate, and named its Caliph: "We clarify to the Muslims that with this declaration of khilafah, it is incumbent upon all Muslims to pledge allegiance to the khalifah Ibrahim and support him (may Allah preserve him). The legality of all emirates, groups, states, and organizations, becomes null by the expansion of the khilafah's authority and arrival of its troops to their areas." Since then, we have seen ISIS become more powerful as it aims to reclaim all lands that were once part of the Ottoman Empire.

ISIS presents a safety risk to those residing in territory within the Ottoman Empire unwilling to convert, whether already some brand of Muslim or of another faith, like Christians. It also presents a strong social media risk with its recruitment program conducted primarily through YouTube, Facebook, and Twitter. On the transactional risk side it depends upon being able to buy and sell oil and move funds inside or outside the financial infrastructure in order to keep up with heavy operational costs of doing business.

A number of countries have signed up to take ISIS on, including the United States and England. Sasha Havlicek of the Institute for Strategic Dialogue, a London- based research organization, noted in a *New York Times* article that reported out on the 60 nation summit held in February that "The problem is that governments are ill placed to lead in the battle of ideas," as she called for private companies to become involved in what she called "the communications problem of our time." [Julie Hirschfield Davis, "Obama Urges Global United Front Against Extremist Groups Like ISIS," *New York Times*, February 18, 2015].

A more recent article in the *Washington Post* suggested that the dream of bringing all Muslims into the Caliphate's tent is eroding rapidly: "Reports of rising tensions between foreign and local fighters, aggressive and increasingly unsuccessful attempts to recruit local citizens for the front lines, and a growing incidence of guerrilla attacks against Islamic State targets suggest the militants are struggling to sustain their carefully cultivated image as a fearsome fighting force drawing Muslims together under the umbrella of a utopian Islamic state."[Liz Sly,"Islamic State appears to be fraying from within," *Washington Post*, March 8, 2015].

So what can we do? In January, hacking group Anonymous declared online war with ISIS. A month later, Anonymous claimed responsibility for targeting nearly 800 Twitter accounts, 12 Facebook pages and over 50 email addresses because of their links with ISIS. Anonymous, a non- nation-state, has also talked about taking down a nation state (Saudi Arabia) because it houses many wealthy donors to ISIS, which would be itself an act of terrorism. Partnering with the NSA to pinpoint ISIS clandestine operations with tools like Google Maps has merit, however, especially on the operational side, for the anti-ISIS coalition. The National Security Administration's cyber ops folks could team up with Anonymous to gather even more data like weapons caches, key individuals, and networks. Such a partnership could avert any claim that Anonymous is not part of a nation state effort. (Just quietly call me to let me know if this coalition is already in action.)

Director of National Intelligence James Clapper estimates in his February report that "Since the conflict began in 2011, more than

20,000 foreign fighters – at least 3,400 of whom are Westerners – have gone to Syria from more than 90 countries." More vigilance by the owners of social media sites like YouTube, Twitter and Facebook can significantly reduce the number of foreigners who join ISIS. Twitter and Facebook have already stepped up to more aggressively suspend the accounts of those sympathetic to or part of ISIS, and it is to be hoped that such efforts, including on YouTube, will be increased. But I suspect more can be done.

The financial risk from a complicated transactional infrastructure that does not look like traditional banking systems has been a real challenge. David Cohen, US Department of Treasury Undersecretary for Terrorism and Financial Intelligence identified the problem in a speech at the Carnegie Endowment for International Peace: "[ISIS] has amassed wealth at an unprecedented pace and its revenue sources have a different composition from those of many other terrorist organizations." It doesn't "depend principally on moving money across international borders," he said, "but obtains the vast majority of its revenues from local criminal and terrorist activities." It's estimated that multiple revenue sources generate up to $6 million a day, sometimes through private donations from rich Mideasterners to alleged charitable or humanitarian organizations, and often through ransoms as well. ISIS middlemen are also expert at using mobile applications to arrange fuel and oil deliveries through the black market.

Clearly new tools and strategies are needed to choke off such lucrative activities that keep ISIS operating on the ground. I recommend a meeting of the best public and private minds to drill down in the two specific operational areas where gaps exist at ISIS: banking and finance, and social media. Unusually sophisticated fringe groups like Anonymous should be invited to the table as well, since they have a great deal of experience in taking down online entities that include ISIS, al-Qaida, and similar groups.

I have not discussed military risk here because I assume that there is a united forces strategy to put an effective fighting force on the ground and in the air, a goal that is still somewhat distant.

Will we always have to talk about ethics?
Issue 42, June 2015

I find that not much has changed where ethics and misconduct are concerned. This article covers both the 2012 and 2015 Labaton Sucharow surveys of the financial services sector in the United States and in the United Kingdom. Other critical infrastructure sectors are not immune from ethical challenges, and are often less regulated than banking.

After the Washington Mutual debacle, I first spoke publicly about ethical misconduct at an enterprise risk management conference in 2012. I was asked by a very angry gentleman what right I had to speak about ethical misconduct when I had been part of the problem at Washington Mutual. I recovered quickly enough from the fierceness of the question to say that I considered myself an expert examiner on this very question now that I had spent three and a half years thinking and studying the question, thinking there might have been some better outcome for investors than the complete loss of their funds that they (and I) had committed to the bank.

From my own experience, the advice I have to give to those whose firm becomes caught up in precarious situations is to ask questions until you get a clear answer from your boss. Ascertain as quickly as possible whether or not your boss is part of a firm's inner circle, shaping the corporate response strategy as pressure mounts. If I could do one thing over, I would set aside a natural professional level of concern that could be satisfied with non-answers like this: "We're working on that right now, and things are looking up." Or "It was an isolated incident and we're putting a new control in place to keep it from happening again." A senior executive's understanding must necessarily be made up of equal parts of industry analysis, concerns from the regulators, and their own expertise in detecting if something is truly wrong. I accepted a range of explanations at Washington Mutual from members of the executive suite that should have suggested they were as uneasy as I was. Because of perceived pressure they appeared to be under, I did not push harder. That is what I would change if I could do things over.

The surveys below indicate just how much people are not usually acting by themselves, but are rather part of a group. I wrote earlier about two rogue traders who felt they had let down, "dishonored" their teams. Often behavior is accepted and questions are not asked when a group's performance is on the line where the annual bonus is concerned. We like to think of ourselves as individual actors who can make decisions that come straight from one's moral compass, but in fact we are sometimes asked to suppress that sense of "the right thing to do" to kept the group as a whole looking good. Add to that the "monkey see/monkey do" behavior to be found in or out of banking firms, and you've a recipe for risk.

I've been looking at the banking and finance sector for a little more than 16 years and I have to say I don't think policy, ethical frameworks, codes of conduct or even regulation has had much of an impact on how employees behave. To satisfy regulators, both before and as a result of Dodd-Frank, firms have created risk units toward the top of the firm which are still frequently confused with internal audit groups rather than embedded in the lines of business. Risk management is perceived by the business as overhead: the cost of doing business, money that could very well have been spent on innovative new products and complex high-speed instruments that will make money out of the gate. Never before has the disparity between those who have and those who are disenfranchised been so great. Here in the US, banks are thriving and, at the same time, lobbying against further limits on their ability to speculate

A *Risk Universe* article in July of 2012 summarised the contents of that year's Labaton Sucharow Financial Services Industry Survey, titled *Wall Street Fleet Street Main Street: Corporate Integrity at a Crossroads*. The study looked at 500 professionals, half from the US and half from the UK. No other study I had read showed with such grim clarity how little impact the financial crisis and subsequent regulatory reforms had on banking behaviour for a statistically significant number of professionals. The report is worth reading still, since there is so much data there, but I find I go back to three pieces of information. First, a staggering number (25% from UK and 22% from the US) felt it was necessary to behave illegally or unethically to get ahead. Second, around 16% "said they would commit a crime, such as insider trading, if they could get away with it". The other significant issue in the 2012 survey was that fear of retaliation for reporting wrongdoing was still very high: "A startling 94% of all professionals surveyed said they would report misconduct if it could be done with a guarantee of anonymity, employment protection and a potential monetary reward".

In the 2012 report, Labaton Sucharow, a well-known firm for its prosecutorial work, concludes: "The best way to ensure the financial marketplace operates with greater transparency, fairness and accountability is to recognise the powerful troika – regulators, corporations and individuals – has the ability to establish and strengthen a culture of integrity that will create lasting change in the financial markets."

Three years later, Labaton Sucharow has released *The Street, The Bull and The Crisis: A Survey of the US & UK Financial Services Industry*. This time, 1,200 professionals in both countries were surveyed, representing "a broad spectrum of the industry, from young professionals to senior executives, investment bankers and investment managers, from San Francisco to Scotland". (2015 report). In this report, we're seeing jumps in statistics when those who make more than $500,000 are reported. In the 2012 survey, 51% of those surveyed in the US were not aware of the SEC Whistleblower Program created by the Dodd- Frank Act, which offers financial compensation for reporting wrongdoing. Education seems to be proceeding at a slug-like pace, since 37% are still unaware of the programme even with this larger number surveyed. There's even more data to sort through this year and here I will highlight ones of particular interest to me. It's pretty clear executives making $500,000 or more are pressured harder to compromise on legal or ethical issues: 23% at the top, compared with 9% who earn less. That same executive group reports having first-hand understanding of wrongdoing at the rate of 34%, compared to 21% who make less. Please note that no matter how you read this report, the percentages are awful for both groups, as are the conclusions those who were surveyed have drawn: 32% believe compensation or bonus plans could cause employees to violate the law or compromise their ethics; 33% of them "feel the industry hasn't changed for the better since the financial crisis". There is significant variance also in the data from those who have been in the industry for many years and those who are relatively new to it. What is new in both cases is the proliferation of agreements – for 25% of those who earn $500,000 or more and for 10% of others – that "would prohibit reporting illegal or unethical activities to the authorities." A significant number of employees (15%-21%) believe their leaders would look the other way if an activity or an individual was driving significant profit. And, in perhaps the most disheartening response of the new survey, 17% of all respondents "find it unlikely company leaders would report misconduct to law enforcement". When they look at regulators and law enforcement bodies in their respective countries, 39% find them ineffective; and that percentage rises to 49% when those who make $500,000 or more are answering.

Individual and corporate integrity are fundamental components of effective risk management. Both studies indicate we have a very long way to go to change the culture inside banking. The C-suite is not making progress on the trust spectrum, or on communicating both values and acceptable behaviour to significantly reduce a firm's losses from fraud or other forms of ethical misconduct. How did we get to a place where doing the right thing (ethics) is perceived by professionals as unprofitable and as grounds for retaliation? So far the troika that Labaton Sucharow spoke about – corporations, regulators and individuals – has been unable to obtain the desired outcome(s).

People should be your greatest asset
Issue 46, October 2015

This short article focuses on four ways employees or contractors increase risk in the workplace, directly or indirectly. Nothing has changed here, but the number of incidents -- from breaches to intellectual property (IP) theft -- has increased as the workplace becomes increasingly complicated. We know from events like the Office of Personnel Management breach, where a third party conducted background checks for top secret clearances, that ancient unpatched software creates opportunities for outside players, and that it takes an exceptionally long time for such breaches to be identified.

What is it that keeps employees and contractors happy in their work and therefore less victim to feelings of being marginalized which in turn opens them up to offers from bad players? We see from the surveys I discuss below that a large number of bankers would perform inside trading if they could not be caught. We know that a bad performance review can cause a disproportionate sense of aggrievement. More recent examples since 2015 can be found on the website of the Carnegie Mellon CERT.

How much privacy should an employee or contractor be given? Most employee agreements indicate that all email belongs to the company, not the individual, and that it can be examined as required. Programs that create an atmosphere of anxiety and paranoia because they allow employees to evaluate one another's performance usually ensure that turnover is high. Such costs should be examined against the cost of replacing an employee and training a new one.

I've written in *The Risk Universe* about people risk before. In November of 2012, I asked about ethical misconduct, in particular from CEOs. I made five recommendations to improve existing programmes and reduce such conduct. Earlier this year, in June, I looked hard at law firm Lobaton Sucharow's surveys of banking professionals, from the first survey in 2012 to the current one this year. The most recent survey was even larger than the first and the results were at least as disappointing as the 2012 results: we see in each that significant numbers of US and UK bankers would engage in insider trading if they thought they would not be caught.

Here I will focus on how managers can manage people risk through a higher level of situational awareness and by being able to identify what has gone wrong and caused financial and/or reputational risk in four different scenarios.

Accidents or mistakes: this is actually the easiest people risk to manage. Should you identify a pattern, you can review your training materials, as well as your policies and procedures and then invest in additional training and clarify your procedures. If the pattern persists, or if the employees making the mistakes are not new employees, then perhaps these are not accidents or mistakes.

Deliberate: Annex 9 of the most recent Basel regulations calls this type of behaviour internal fraud: "Losses due to acts of a type intended to defraud, misappropriate property, or circumvent regulations, the law or company policy... "This covers a lot of ground. Such fraud can be reduced by investing up front during the hiring process in background checks, particularly if there are aberrations in the employment history which need to be checked. We know from the detailed research which the Carnegie Mellon University CERT Division has carried out, that managers should be especially alert when an employee's performance is downgraded and the employee feels unappreciated. If such a person has development and/or administrative privileges, the results can be very expensive for the firm. The same applies to an employee one is terminating: be sure both network and remote access are terminated. (I know, that sounds very simplistic, yet there is a whole study done by the CERT and the Secret Service who interviewed former banking employees now in jail and you would be surprised how often that might have happened: the former employee went home and still had remote access open by which damage could be done.)

Third parties: Here, the people committing the fraud or property misappropriation are contractors and vendors. I wrote about vendor risk and intellectual property in November of 2013. I am not sure the situation has improved since, unless the firm has seen a significant loss because of access that a contractor or vendor had to facilities and/or records. The Carnegie Mellon CERT has written extensively on this type of risk as well. In point of fact, we don't do well at ensuring our contractors are walled off well enough inside our production systems (example: Target Corporation and access obtained by hackers through an HVAC vendor's credentials). Again, here we recommend good solid background checks on vendors along with detailed binding clauses in contracts signed. I would recommend each contract contain a list of subcontractors that the contractor signing the contract may be using; and the same type of background investigations conducted on the subcontractors. Then monitor your critical vendors closely.

Social media: These days every employee is a potential commentator on social media unless there is a clear policy in place which outlines what's acceptable and what is not. Are they allowed to comment on their workday? On their manager? On their company? Policies and laws may vary by sector or country. It is worthwhile to develop a clear policy that is not inconsistent with brand statements so employees do not inadvertently hurt the company when they are anxious or tired. Out of a turbulent last several years, the Seattle Police Department developed a comprehensive social media policy of many parts. Here is a small but relevant portion of the policy as it applies to officers: "The Department recognises the role that social media plays in the personal lives of some Department employees. However, the personal use of social media can have bearing on employees in their official capacity as they are held to a high standard by the community. Engaging in prohibited speech outlined in this policy may provide grounds for discipline and may be used to undermine or impeach an officer's testimony in legal proceedings."

A few words as I close about attempts using technology to build the "better mousetrap by which to catch them" that employee surveillance programmes use – ranging from the software which the trading desks have used for several years on traders' email; or the type of new surveillance software JPMorgan Chase announced in its annual report last year; or the creepy software which some multinational corporations currently use, where employees can report on other employees, with or without cause. Are employees aware such programmes are being used? Does that make them more or less anxious, more or less willing to cheat if they think they can get away with it? Given a range of options in the marketplace, do people want to work for companies that deploy such tools? Only time and a bit more transparency about what is actually done with the data which is collected will tell. Hire the right people and your need for such technology decreases. Inspire them to do the right thing and you probably cut the risk still further.

A chance for bankers to step forward
Issue 49, January 2016

The Islamic State (ISIS) continues to operate in the Mideast, and convert Europeans and others to its cause via the Internet. While advances and retreats take place in Iraq and Syria, single actors use trucks, cars, bombs and suicide vest to create climates of fear across Europe and America in particular. Taking down the Internet platform could go a long way to reducing the flow of donations and exchanges of cash on the Dark Web. Pairing Anonymous with the National Security Agency still seems like a possible strategy.. Reducing the amount of land held reduces the amount of taxes collected or sales from oil and agricultural products. But the question remains: if not ISIS, then is Al-Qaeda still a force to be reckoned with? Is there still a role that bankers can play in the flow of mercenaries' money in the Mideast? Smart bankers might be our greatest asset if allowed to take ISIS and Al-Qaeda on.

When I wrote here in February 2015, I suggested the National Security Agency (NSA) could partner with activist group Anonymous, or similar fringe groups, to cut off the flow of money to and from the Islamic State (IS, ISIS, ISIL or Daesh). Anonymous at that time had already been at work identifying Twitter accounts, which recruited for Daesh and getting Twitter to shut them down. It appears somewhat the same arrangement might have been in place for Facebook accounts, which lured recruits with videos and other marketing materials to show off the advantages of joining the movement. Those are both different efforts than I was discussing, which might in fact interfere with pre-existing law enforcement investigations, where sites have been left up and active by law enforcement to gain even more intelligence on the next steps of terrorists.

I am still looking for an alignment of agencies and independent organisations, which would actively seek to cut the flow of money coming from sales of oil, agricultural products or taxes imposed in Iraq and Syria in particular, whether they are conducted on the surface internet or on the dark web using Tor encryption.

Why should bankers care? Surely we have enough regulations already, forcing us to identify and report suspicious activity, patterns and movements of money under, for example, the Anti Money Laundering (AML) Act in the US, or the 3rd European Council Directive on "prevention of the use of the financial system for the purpose of money laundering and terrorist financing". We are at a remarkable point in time where banking is concerned. Though currency has always been moved outside formal entities like banks, bankers internationally suffer a tarnished reputation these days, especially as we continue to see fines paid for outrageous behaviour, not all of which is connected with the 2008 financial crisis. Add to that data from two Labaton Sucharow studies, which I have previously written about, indicating many bankers would engage in insider trading if they could get away with it; and a full 23% of executives making $500,000 or more are pressured to compromise on legal or ethical issues. It's time to take significant action to improve the reputation of the banking profession – and the current world crisis with Daesh offers a clear-cut opportunity.

Bankers should care because, in previous times of war and profiteering, banks looked the other way. Despots paid significant fees to stash their money in secure and confidential numbered accounts in countries with strong bank secrecy laws, like Switzerland, Lebanon, Singapore and Luxembourg, as well as offshore banks and other tax havens under voluntary or statutory privacy provisions.

So let's use the profiling tools which help us report suspicious activity in new ways. Let's allocate time each day to turn our corporate information security people loose on the dark web, the place which *Bright Planet* describes as "intentionally hidden and … inaccessible through standard web browsers". Though it's not clear what they will find, it is known Daesh used Bitcoin for transactions until that system became unreliable. What we are looking for is where the money is stored: is Daesh money in sharia bank accounts, or stashed in caves in the Middle East?

Or invested in halaal industries around the world? Or buried in numbered accounts in Swiss and other banks? I believe it is in our best interests to move into a proactive stance, partnering where possible with law enforcement; and that such an effort could be led by the European Union and the US. Certainly since the November 13th Paris attack, relations between intelligence organisations have improved significantly. The goal is to block or eliminate the flow of money over the surface web, as well as on the dark web.

It's clear, as long as the money continues to flow, financial institutions need to take extraordinary precautions to protect their people and their facilities. Though banks are not normally considered 'soft targets', like those in Paris and Beirut, there is no doubt, from terrorist advisories written more than a decade ago, the goal is to destroy "abomination and perversion". For commentary on the immediate lessons from the Paris attack, as well as a summary of what to do in the case of an attack on your facility, read Peter Power's excellent piece for *Continuity Central*. For those who might have doubts about whether Daesh is a passing fad, it is instructive to look at a few declarative statements from Islamic extremists. Following the 2005 London subway bombing, an al-Qaeda spokesman said "Our religion is Islam, obedience to the one true god and following the footsteps of the final prophet messenger. Your democratically- elected governments continuously perpetuate atrocities against my people all over the world." Nine years later, Abu Bakr al-Baghdadi declared himself caliph of all 1.8bn Muslims, calling on them to gather to his new land and unite to "capture Rome" and own the world.

In a momentous piece in *Le Monde* earlier this month, Turkish Islamic scholar Fethullah Gulen called on Muslims to review their understanding of Islam and to step forward to fully participate "to tackle the violent extremism problem in all its dimensions: political, economic, social and religious". If becoming more proactive as a profession in the face of such evil is practical for financial institutions, then it is as well that we find new ways to reach into Muslim communities and to partner with them in this effort, overcoming historic distrust of our institutions and standing firm in our commitment to one another.

The encryption dustup
Issue 52, April 2016

The tension between surveillance and privacy, between law and policy, between data confidentiality and access is as old as time. Whether or not we can remain constant to certain principles in time of war (or what is perceived as war by the government) is what is at stake in this 2016 attempt by the Federal Bureau of Investigation to compel computer manufacturer Apple to create a "backdoor" into its newest encrypted smartphone for law enforcement. Apple had begin to encrypt customer data so not even they had access to it, though the company had cooperated in earlier versions of the device to unlock the data for law enforcement. FBI director James Comey argued that encryption made it harder for law enforcement to solve cases. Apple argued that the government was trying to deprive the company of liberty and due process. Undoubtedly the argument will come up again and we will see the Trump administration double down on Apple and other technology firms, who are only beginning to understand the unholy alliance that a federal contract brings under this administration. It is still worth it to read the full version of Apple's eloquently written brief to the court, since moot when the FBI withdrew its case, noting that it had been able to find another party willing to break into the phone.

"There is nothing new in the realization that the Constitution sometimes insulates the criminality of a few in order to protect the privacy of us all."
            – U.S. Supreme Court Justice Antonin Scalia, 1987

Though the US Department of Justice withdrew its request of Apple, Inc. on March 21, there is no doubt that it, or some other international government agency, will be back to request that a technology provider creates a back door into its encrypted software so the government might read the content on a suspect digital device. Legislation to compel technology companies is already under discussion in both England and France. In France's Digital Republic amendment: "Manufacturers of IT equipment – phones, tablets, computers – are gradually moving toward individual encryption of devices out of a desire to protect their users' personal data...This move is virtuous for protecting personal data. However, it has a downside when faced with the need for the protection and security of the state."

In the proposed French legislation, which has been on the table since earlier terrorist attacks in Paris, companies that do not comply could face up to five years in prison and a roughly US$400,000 fine. [Joshua Eaton, "With or without evidence, terrorism fuels combustible encryption debate," *Christian Science Monitor*, March 29, 2016.] In the UK, prime minister David Cameron has asked for a ban on encrypted applications that do not offer a back door to law enforcement authorities with a warrant. Undoubtedly, the desire to move such legislation forward will become more intense after recent horrific bombings in Brussels, Baghdad and Lahore. Despite the fact most reports indicate the terrorists in Brussels were using disposable phones and text messages, not an encrypted application like WhatsApp, relationships between governments and the private sector are likely to become more strained as we go forward. It is worth also noting that the failure to find any messaging by terrorists does not automatically mean there must have been encrypted messages, no matter what the current political climate in these three countries might suggest.

The European Commission is working to further refine data protection laws in the European Union, but as they stand, those laws are far more definitive than the Bill of Rights which privacy advocates in the US stand on, which could generally be summarised as the privacy of beliefs, speech and the press (First Amendment); privacy of the home against demands that it be used to house soldiers (Third Amendment); the privacy of the person and possessions as against unreasonable searches, which includes both the evidence of "probable cause" and the use of a warrant (Fourth Amendment); and the Fifth Amendment's privilege against self-incrimination, which provides protection for the privacy of personal information.

In the motion to vacate the government's order, filed by Apple in late February, Apple took the following position with respect to being ordered to write code that would break encryption: "This amounts to compelled speech and viewpoint discrimination in violation of the First Amendment...Under well-settled law, computer code is treated as speech within the meaning of the First Amendment...The Supreme Court has made clear that where, as here, the government seeks to compel speech, such actions trigger First Amendment protections."

Apple also argued: "In addition to violating the First Amendment, the government's requested order, by conscripting a private party with an extraordinarily attenuated connection to the crime to do the government's bidding in a way that is statutorily unauthorised, highly burdensome and contrary to the party's core principles, violates Apple's substantive due process right to be free from 'arbitrary deprivation of [its] liberty by government.'"

We will see these arguments made again, on both sides of the ocean, in legislative chambers and in the press. Apple points out that "examples abound of society opting not to pay the price for increased and more efficient enforcement of criminal laws," which brings us full circle back to Justice Scalia's point that the defence of privacy will sometimes mean criminals are not caught.

Clearly technology has created useful tools for law enforcement over the past several centuries. But the tools were not necessarily created for law enforcement. Cameras were created to record life and events, though some thought them at the time to be an unreasonable violation of privacy. The telephone led not only to streamlined communications but eventually to wiretaps of the highest fidelity. Mobile phone towers/sites created a range of peripheral products, including the StingRay device now quietly used by a wide variety of law enforcement agencies. As devices got smaller and more portable, the ability to retain vast amounts of information grew. In the US, the Supreme Court ruled not long ago that a warrant is required to search a smartphone, just like it is required to search a computer. Both pieces of technology contain not only our email, or our contacts, but also photos we may wish to keep private and messages created out of convenience with an assumption we are using a secure device. Apple and other manufacturers have moved to encrypt our data for us so they are not responsible for it, especially so (given what we know from Edward Snowden's release of classified documents) the government can no longer request our information from them, with or without a warrant. That is what is at the heart of this issue. Operational risks abound, both from the privacy side and in terms of citizens' security, particularly in our ability to live our lives without fear in public places. I would rather see law enforcement acquire better predictive tools than watch them compel global technology companies to deliberately build in back doors to systems or applications we purchase because we believe they are secure. No matter how many attacks we suffer, this issue is not going away, neither in America nor Europe.

Can the centre hold?
Issue 56, August 2016

Since I wrote this column, foreign and domestic tensions have only increased, especially where cyber attacks conducted by nation states and terrorism as exemplified in real world lone wolf scenarios are concerned. Extremism is on the rise in this country and abroad. Though some studies have shown that law enforcement officers wearing body cameras does not change behavior significantly, we do observe a larger number of officers now being fired after body or dashboard video is examined. Globally, relationships with historic allies have been undercut by this administration, both at a treaty level and in terms of ongoing trade relations.. The tensions are not just political: the workplace has become the political base of millennials seeking to effect change in the policies and practices of their employers where contract work with the public sector is concerned. Employees at Google and Microsoft have petitioned their employers to withdraw from contracts that aid (for example) government surveillance through facial recognition or drone targeting programs. The advice I offer toward the end of this column about how firms can protect their employees can be supplemented today -- after the u.tube employee recreational area incident -- by advising that protections begin at the perimeter of a corporate property, not just in the private areas of the building itself where access is regulated.

These first three lines of a poem that Yeats wrote after the first world war resonate with us today and have been referenced in American political debate – and perhaps also around the Brexit vote as well. Going it alone or going it together with other countries appears at least to be the question as discord and violence present themselves more regularly, in no small part because of the technology now available to us.

I've spent the past month writing about conduct risk, in particular about what I see as the top three root causes in banking: tone at the top; culture; and conflicts of interest. But as events continue to unfold, I see parallels in the real world, in particular around the two faces of technology, best illustrated by looking at some of those events.

In the world of cyber, two types of attacks appear pervasive: ones committed by nation-state players for objectives not always clear to us, but certainly to unsettle governments; and those committed by criminals driven by lucrative benefits around breaches, whether it's the sale of intellectual property, ransom demands to critical infrastructure firms, or the skimming off and sale of customer data.

Terrorism has added a frantic layer to our discussions. In this year alone, starting in March, suicide, active shooters and car bombings that had once occurred primarily in the Middle East moved into Europe and America again, starting with Brussels in March, then Orlando in June, then Germany and France again in July. At the same time, police in Dallas and New Orleans have been murdered, contributing further to the sense that things are out of control, that the centre will not hold.

Never before have international law enforcement officials been under so much pressure to reduce the incidence of unpredictable lone wolf attacks and to make communities safe once again for their citizens. More police departments are choosing to arm their officers with body cameras and, in some cases, with military body armour. At the same time, intelligence agencies like MI6 and the FBI are pursuing leads that point to both hackers and terrorists. Since the groups committing unspeakable acts are not traditionally organised and are, in more cases, self-radicalised from social media and other technology platforms, preventative or anticipatory intelligence efforts depend even more heavily upon technology, whether CCTV or active monitoring efforts of certain urban conclaves.

At the same time, privacy rules abroad are tightening, especially since the latest opinion by the European Data Protection Supervisor. Here in the US, the FBI director has called for a robust discussion around encryption before the next terrorist event occurs; and, as indicated in an earlier column, the government's surveillance powers have been increased in both England and France. In the US, a whole political party has been taken over by a businessman whose rhetoric and careless promises remind us of earlier years in Germany and the rise of fascism.

What exactly can financial organisations do to keep their people safe and confident in their work, especially if based in France or Belgium – or even England? From our operational risk practices, we know that it is not possible to avoid all risk. But it is possible for firms to hold special training sessions for their employees that cover topics like active shooters and situational awareness. Some of this is common sense, but there are additional lessons to be learned from recent events. Firms may wish to harden their infrastructures even further and add a layer or two of physical security for employees. Business travellers should continue to expect delays, as governments determine what other measures they might put in place. Learning to be situationally aware is perhaps the next highest priority, especially if attending large public gatherings like sporting events, or parades, or other types of places where one must stand in line to enter. We know that terrorists have also effectively used public transportation systems and places of worship in addition to open air markets and restaurants.

Visual scans of your environment for suspicious behaviour and/or packages is important. Being exhorted to be careful may be uncomfortable, but it is necessary. Just as we say "Think before you click" to employees about their email, "If you see something, say something" is a good mantra. There is always the possibility of hysterical finger-pointing. Efforts to remain calm and observational are hampered in both the US and Europe right now by the political rhetoric of fear-mongering. We have certainly seen some of that with air travellers in the US, who have insisted that certain passengers be removed if they speak another language or dress in their native garb. But I believe it's possible to settle in to practiced observation and reflection on what has become an uncertain world. Law enforcement alone cannot make us safe. We must do all that we can, together, to make the conditions in which we live and work less risky. In part, that means putting away our smartphones and looking about us with new eyes. Yes, that means being more careful – but it also offers an opportunity to see that for which we should be grateful every day.

When does 'taking full responsibility' have consequences?
Issue 58, October 2016

Has there ever been a CEO who, when appearing in front of shareholders or boards of directors, or Congress, does not say "I take full responsibility for this problem?" For many years, under the guise of lawyerly advice as well as directors and officers insurance, there have been basically no consequences for problematic CEOs except perhaps termination and some level of clawback on future options. Since I wrote this in 2016, a number of additional issues have come to light at Wells Fargo, the current poster child for failed governance and an absence of meaningful internal controls. Additional fines, including one in the amount of $1billion in February of 2018, have been leveraged, along with an injunction that Wells replace four board members. The Federal Reserve in the same order has restricted Wells' assets to $2trillion, its size at the end of 2017, until it can clean up its internal controls and compliance processes. The severity of the actions by the Fed is in part because the problems at Wells have been found to extend past the community banking division, into its business division as well as its wealth management programs.

Should the firm have cleaned house and brought in an outside CEO to replace John Stumpf, rather than promoting the former president and COO, Timothy Sloan? Despite slick double-page advertising spreads that purport to show all the reforms that the firm has made, Sloan struggles still to impose the type of discipline and transparency that regulators are looking for. Risk management is still clearly an issue at Wells. By restricting the firm's growth, the Fed hopes to show the firm just how serious regulators are about consequences of misconduct at all levels of the firm.

Rarely has there been such lag time between the onset of a high risk event and executive consequences, as we've recently seen in the case of Wells Fargo. The bank's conduct risk issues took several years to be acted upon, with a cast of characters that included a *Los Angeles Times* reporter, the Consumer Financial Protection Bureau (CFPB), the State of California, the US Senate and House Banking Committees and the bank's board of directors. In the US, quarterly Sarbanes Oxley Act (SOX) financial reporting by publically traded corporations to the Securities and Exchange Commission (SEC) under Section 302 can be broken down into three areas: an accurate and fair presentation of the reporting and its disclosures; attestation on well-established and maintained disclosure controls and procedures; and reporting of deficiencies in, and changes to, internal accounting controls. In other words, "A. all significant deficiencies in the design or operation of internal controls which could adversely affect the issuer's ability to record, process, summarise, and report financial data and have identified for the issuer's auditors any material weaknesses in internal controls; and B. any fraud, whether or not material, that involves management or other employees who have a significant role in the issuer's internal controls;" [Section 302, Numbers 5A and 5B]

We can count the number of quarters Wells Fargo executives failed to report accounting control deficiencies based on fraudulent activity to boost sales numbers around cross sells. Executives sailed along for nearly three years under this cross-sell programme, established by the former CEO and cheerfully upheld by the current CEO, as reports should have accrued on why employees were fired and what corrective action(s) needed to be taken.

How is it that, after a 2013 *Los Angeles Times* investigative report on fraudulent practices at Wells Fargo was published, both John Stumpf, the bank's chief executive officer and Carrie Tolstedt, its former head of community banking, did not respond and report the scale of the problem? Where was internal audit, external audit, regulators or the board of directors? In a *New York Times* article titled 'Policing the banks is an inside job', Jordan Thomas argues we need better pathways at the regulatory level for whistleblowing; while a day later Gretchen Morgenson illustrates just how rare it is for boards of directors to claw back pay or stock from problematic executives in a column titled 'Executive pay clawbacks are gratifying, but not particularly effective'. Though the SEC has a relatively successful whistleblower programme in place, none of the regulatory agencies really do. It seems that none of the 5,000+ employees fired by Wells Fargo for following orders had an appeals process external to the bank. Retaliation appears to have been a standard practice: those who tried to report the fraudulent activity to human resources (HR) or via an anonymous ethics hotline found that it was not so anonymous when they were fired. On the clawback issue, even though firms are now encouraged but not required to have their own internal (rarely utilised) clawback policies, Morgenson points out that on the regulatory side: "Even with its prosecutorial power, the SEC has brought just 40 cases against top executives since 2011. Only 18 of those have generated cash payments from executives; some U$17m was returned to their companies. (Many of the cases are still being litigated.)"

The US$185m fine makes a very small dent on Wells Fargo's US$23bn in earnings last year. The US$2.6m returned to customers whose identities were used to open fraudulent accounts is likewise just a small ripple on a very large surface. The estimated US$60m in unvested stock options clawed back from the two executives is also only a modest dent in future earnings. Though congressional committees called for the resignation of the CEO – and for sheer oration, I recommend the remarks of US Senator Elizabeth Warren – it should be noted it took the Senate Banking Committee's questioning of Stumpf to prod the Wells Fargo board of directors into action that led to the clawbacks on bonuses, base salaries and Tolstedt's exit pay. Even more surprising, the very cross-sell practices that had led to the fines were still in place when Stumpf's first round of testimony took place. By the time he came back to appear in front of the House Banking Committee, he was able to announce that the cross-sell goal would be scrapped not at the end of 2016, but at the end of the week.

So what are we to make of this particular series of events? Firstly, it goes without saying that most large firms (not just Wells Fargo) have not yet managed to create policies and programmes which reward compliance to regulations, establish safe pathways for those who have thought about reporting wrongdoing, or which truly hold those at the top to the same behavioural standards as those on the front line. It is said that Wells Fargo prided itself on its 'Main Street' reputation, on its distance from Wall Street fraud and 2008 economic woes. Morgenson points out that the board of directors clawed back on the basis of damage to Wells Fargo's reputation. I have argued elsewhere that there are three root causes of conduct risk: tone at the top (check), corporate culture (check) and conflicts of interest (check). Yes, they all play out in this example. If you set the cross-sell goal at the top, that's part of the tone you set for all employees and you should probably continuously monitor what consequences that goal produces (how much staff turnover, of which how many were firings? How often are sales goals exceeded? What's the role of the manager in meeting the sales goal? How often are managers reported to the 'anonymous' ethics line?). In his senate testimony, Stumpf said over and over what an ethical culture the bank had established. Obviously he had not been asking any of the questions I outlined above. Finally, conflicts of interest abound in such a pressure cooker. From the employee's perspective, the daily hectoring from the manager on how much had been accomplished that day or that week is not necessarily an incentive to do more or better. Being required to stay after hours or work on weekends to support the overall sales goal should be a large flag but could easily be interpreted as professional failing. Finally, hearing about others being fired for reporting irregularities is not an incentive to report them.

Last but certainly not least, where was the board of directors? What types of reports were its members reviewing since 2013? Had they read the investigative article when it was published, and did it prompt them to ask any questions of the CEO, himself a member of the board? There were several former regulators on the board; did the full board review the quarterly reports or the 10K statement? I suspect there will be some fine-tuning of regulatory guidance after the Wells Fargo drama, but it is hard not to conclude this is not a one-off instance and we have still not managed, neither in guidance nor in the character of our banking leaders, to clean up practices which feed the bottom line but are just plain wrong.

History is always being made
Issue 60, December 2016

If one theme runs through my writing, it is the exhortation for citizens to register to vote and then to vote consistently, understanding that that is the basis of representation at all levels of government, including the federal government. Since late January of 2017, we've had to live with federal leadership that is chaotic and divisive. It is difficult to separate their political determination to reduce government bureaucracy and reverse the policies and programs of the previous administration from their lack of public service experience. Whole websites for agencies have been decimated. Vacant positions at (for example) the U.S. State Department have not been filled. Interestingly enough, the one cabinet position that has remained stable for the past 18 months is that of the Secretary of the Treasury, whom I discuss in the article. There has been a significant amount of planned and unplanned turnover across the executive branch. Many career diplomats are close to resigning or retiring because public service has become devalued, both by the administration and by the general public.

The brightest light on the horizon is the movement begun by Parkland High School Students that includes a traveling road campaign this summer to register to vote their fellow high school students who have turned 18 years of age. This is not an insignificant number of potential voters, especially when added to the 80-90 million citizens who did not vote in the 2016 presidential election. Their actions are focused on voting out Congressional representatives who are comfortable with the few current gun control measures in place, and who are financed in their re-election campaigns by the National Rifle Association (NRA). If we are ever to see a course correction from the direction the country took during the election, we have to see in first in the ballot box, as well as in protests and street demonstration. Lasting change comes through exercise of one's right and privilege to vote.

For many of us, the past 50 or so years have looked like slow but steady progress under both US political parties on issues such as life, liberty, equality and the pursuit of happiness. Another way to measure that progress is to note that no new US constitutional amendments have been offered in the past 24 years. In the past five years, technology's advances have meant that citizens have become reporters – and sometimes recorders – of social injustices that have yet to be resolved. Another phenomena called "false news" has become more prevalent due to the use of social media platforms. Come January, based upon president-elect Trump's statements and the cabinet level nominations he has made to date, it appears to me that Americans will be citizens of a kakistocracy (Greek: κακιστοκρατία; kækɪsˈtɑkɹəsi) – which Oxford Dictionaries defines as "government by the least suitable or competent citizens of a state." Though I am trying to keep an open mind, it is hard to do so when many cabinet posts are being filled by former military generals or by private sector persons with either no record of public service, or with an attitude that foreshadows dismantling a range of government programmes.

We have yet to understand just where the nominee for treasury secretary will fall. Like several secretaries who precede him, Steve Mnuchin is a former Goldman Sachs partner, currently chief executive of Dune Capital Management, a privately-owned hedge fund. According to the *New York Times*, he "was involved deeply in developing the president- elect's tax proposals, which could deliver as much as US$6tn in tax reductions over 10 years but might also contribute to much larger budget deficits. As treasury secretary, he would take a lead role in developing policies aimed at boosting the country's economic growth." Mnuchin may also be remembered as the guy who put together a group of investors to purchase IndyMac in 2009 in a deal with the Federal Deposit Insurance Corporation (FDIC). The group renamed the bank and proceeded to foreclose on roughly 30,000 homeowners. Whether he will have the patience to listen to the large banks, to understand if they really do want to roll back Dodd-Frank regulations given the investments they have made to reduce the risk of failing, will be an early indicator of what we might see in the way of actual policy. Fortunately, the Treasury Department is stocked with career professionals who have served under both Republicans and Democrats. Let us hope they will stay in their jobs.

At stake in the government's relationship with the private sector are such fundamental principles as that of separation of powers, of separation between church and state, the role of a free press, the First Amendment rights to free speech and freedom to worship (which includes all worship, including that of Muslims); and the Fourth Amendment requirements for probable cause and use of a warrant to search a citizen.

Somewhat moderating such risks are the heavy weight of bureaucracy and the difficulty of enacting actual change at the federal government level, as well as the system of checks and balances that has existed in this country since its inception, a system one hopes will hold up on issues such as the US Army Corps of Engineers' recent denial of an easement to allow a pipeline to be constructed half a mile from the reservation of the Standing Rock Sioux, whose members are concerned that a pipeline breach could threaten their drinking water and sacred Native American sites. President-elect Trump has indicated he will want to review that decision, so it is entirely possible that a reversal of that decision by Trump will end up in front of federal courts – which is why most of the Native Americans and the several thousand US veterans who have arrived to protect them will probably stay in place for several more months, despite horrible weather conditions.

At a federal policy level, emerging risks include the elimination of current executive orders on the first day of the new president's term; a gutting of the role of the Department of Justice's consent orders with local police departments in existence in cities that needed them; the repeal of the current federal health insurance programme; and similar gutting of other cabinet roles where it is felt that the government has over-reached. Certainly there will be a move to appoint a Supreme Court justice quickly, with an eye to throwing out some of our most important protections for women's right to choose.

Through all of this we see that the impact of all these actions will fall most heavily on our most disenfranchised and profiled members: immigrants, Muslims (or those who look like they are Muslims), the LGBQ community and other minorities such as Native Americans and African Americans. It will almost certainly be the case that the national security and surveillance apparatus first implemented after 9/11, since strengthened and enhanced by the current administration, will grow substantially, targeting those I've already identified.

The lesson for Americans in this past election should be that so many of our citizens, 80-90 million of them, decided not to exercise their right to vote, for a variety of reasons, or perhaps for no reason at all. That's a risk we can't afford to take again. If nothing else, effective risk management must include a return to educating each citizen about her/his right to vote; and a better understanding of what government can or can't fix.

"Why didn't we see this one coming?"
Issue 63, March 2017

As in a number of these articles, I'm looking here at how information travels up the corporate decision-making chain. In this article and the next, I'm focused on whether or not a risk management operation can track the flow of information, in order to track whether or not complete information is being received by the governors, whether in the C-suite or in the boardroom. I have previously discussed how executives frequently do not want all the details, how in fact as one rises up the management chain there is an expectation that a good leader keeps her/his hands off the operation itself. If we spent nearly the amount of time on teaching potential leaders how to ask hard questions as we do on how to keep their hands off operations, we would be better off in every respect. In both the public and private sector, it's important to keep a kind of Rumsfeldian list of what we don't know and what we are nonetheless worried about. This is one of the gifts that a strong risk management program brings to the corporate table when strategy is being discussed.

I led two conduct risk workshops on March 13 in New York City that preceded the Operational Risk North America conference which should have begun on March 14 but got cancelled because of a severe winter storm. In the first workshop, I looked at the root causes of conduct risk – tone at the top, culture and conflicts of interest – and in all types of companies, not just banks. In the second workshop, I analysed Wells Fargo and Washington Mutual, as prime examples not only of operational risk failures, but also of conduct risk. Throughout the day, participants, who included both regulators and international bankers, searched for signs, other than those produced by standard risk assessment and reporting, of imminent conduct risk failures. And isn't that the question that most of us have when we look back to try to understand why costly failures were not caught? Why didn't we see this one coming?

Once a robust risk management programme is rolled out in a firm, it should complement what the other two lines of defence are identifying – but it should also be positioned for proactive identification of outliers and/or anomalies. As former US secretary of defence Donald Rumsfeld once so inelegantly said: "There are known knowns. There are things we know that we know. There are known unknowns. That is to say, there are things that we know we don't know. But there are also unknown unknowns. There are things we don't know we don't know." What Rumsfeld left out of this lit are the things we know we don't want to know more about.

How does that work, you might well ask? Without going into a great deal of detail, it's easy to see that a board of directors or even the CEO and CFO might prefer not to be briefed on the means used to deliver wallopingly large profits. At Wells Fargo, when standard sales pitches could not do the trick, employees resorted to using customer data to create additional accounts or services to hit the "eight is great"goal on cross-selling. Quotas were monitored daily, and employees understood from observing their managers and other employees that if they did not make their goal, they would have to work nights and weekends to hit the goal. It is estimated that a total of 2.1 million accounts were opened without the customer's permission. Assuming there was a risk management organisation present and that some form of balanced scorecard was presented to the executive suite and to the board of directors, how is it possible that the firing of 5,300 employees for "improper conduct" over five years was not significant enough to register on the radar of the board of directors? The irony is, of course, that revenue did not actually grow that significantly from this retail group misconduct. After former CEO John Stumpf and retail banking head Carrie Tolstedt had retired and had their bonuses clawed back last fall, Wells recently fired four senior managers in the retail group. The corrective action comes three to four years after the *Los Angeles Times* printed an investigatory piece on the practices. The question remains whether or not the board of directors did not see this one coming.

Are there other key risk indicators that could have been established at either Wells Fargo or Washington Mutual?

That would of course presume that there was someone in charge who could have read and interpreted the warning signs present in such a report. It is still too easy to look the other way when profits are flowing or (as in the case of Washington Mutual) executives believe they have managed all the threats sufficiently to survive. At Washington Mutual, toward the end, risk reporting was debunked and ignored. The chief risk officer who had tried to reason with the C-suite was fired the morning after he met with a board member. (I dislike telling that story to my students because it is a graphic illustration of the point that delivering negative risk news is not necessarily a rewarding activity for a risk manager.) I suspect that many other banks have boards and C-suite executives who are also capable of ignoring risk indicators and/or firing the messenger. As we also saw at Washington Mutual, those who had historically delivered reliable information – the former CFO and the former chief credit officer, each in turn move into the position of chief risk officer until they retired or withdrew to an "advisory" position, no longer part of the executive committee – were sidelined or eliminated in order to put more risk on the balance sheet and to ignore certain information that they were producing as part of their job. It's easy enough to see in retrospect. But, as far as I know, there is not a way to produce a key risk indicator for greed, dishonesty, avarice and outsized ambition.

Executives and risk: what your teams won't tell you
Issue 66, June 2017

I once thought I could write a whole book on executives and risk, that would examine operational risk and the challenge of information flow up the management chain. I organized the material I thought I could cover using examples from four critical information sectors, and intending to ground my research by interviewing at least one CEO in each of those sectors. I have since concluded that any book I might write would take my attention away from real time historic events that provide almost continuous examples for students of methodologies and frameworks. Technology and technology companies, indeed most of our information technology infrastructure is evolving so rapidly as to make such a book outdated before it could be published.

Sometimes good risk management is simply looking beyond the end of your nose, and asking what could go wrong if you accepted a recommendation from one of your teams. For every new layer of strategic planning, this sort of risk analysis is required -- from the board, from your own executive team, and from lower level managers, who often have more detailed information than you have been presented with.

Finally, the penultimate question: under what conditions would it make sense to modify or veto this recommendation?

There are so many global risks that present themselves today, it is difficult to select a topic for a *Risk Universe* swan song – but first my thanks to publisher Mike Finlay and editors Victoria Tozer-Pennington and Carrie Cook for a great run over the past five years.

Operational risk management is still a relatively new discipline. Like other disciplines that have evolved in a complex technological world, the maturity of practitioners varies widely. In the past nine or so years, as companies have spun out of control, we've seen corporate managers rebrand themselves into this field or get promoted into it without necessarily understanding risk frameworks or methodologies. There is a great deal of variation in the maturity of established risk programmes inside large companies and in where such a programme is housed organisationally.

Risk management differs from audit or compliance management in that it has forward-looking, strategic, business intelligence components. It does not simply measure what is already in place with an eye to finding deficiencies. In this sense, it most closely resembles programmes like information security or business continuity, which have both forward-looking assessment and operational elements for dealing with corporate disruptions. Tools like information security's threat analysis and business continuity's business impact analysis can provide some key building blocks for an operational risk programme. Both tools rely upon a close and keen understanding of critical business processes within a company and are designed to track interdependencies and impacts. Many firms now have risk management programmes in place, but still experience financial losses that are a direct result of failures in people, processes, systems or external events. How can executives best utilise the risk management programmes they already have in place? Or improve them?

Executives are often the last to know what might go wrong inside their companies. The larger the company, the greater the level of complexity – and the greater the possibility that teams from audit or compliance programmes really only report what they observe at the time of the audit, or reprise what they have seen in the past. Auditors and regulators frequently have an outdated understanding of technology and/or products based upon new innovations in technology. Look how long it took regulators to understand cloud computing, which American regulators identified initially as just another kind of vendor risk. Though training for regulators has increased, it is still difficult to understand evolving technologies and practices such as high-speed trading instruments, or even how a ransomware attack works. Compliance personnel are concerned with the strict interpretation and reporting of compliance to the law. Add to that studies that show how disaffected most employees are from their companies and what you have is an elevated level of risk that may not be auditable and may not yet constitute a compliance issue. It is not necessarily that teams don't report elevated levels of risk, so much as it is that the forms of analysis and protocols for reporting by auditors and/or regulators make it almost impossible for an executive to ask the right question of his/her team(s). So where is the information bottleneck?

Boards of directors hire chief executive officers (CEOs) who share certain leadership characteristics, around which hundreds of *Harvard Business Review* articles are written. Certainly, experience counts, but because of privacy protections, liability questions and complex exit agreements, recruiters for other firms are probably not made aware of issues or remediation plans that the candidate may have experienced in previous engagements. We've seen that extreme self-confidence goes a long way in the boardroom and inside the company. Most C-suite executives have made their reputations by making bold (testerical) decisions and taking a significant amount of risk. In technology firms, often the CEO is one of the founders of the company and a different set of behaviours is required for the entrepreneur than for the CEO. In some cases, a failure by a new CEO to assume the mantle of gravitas and shed testerical behaviour causes a problem in the firm's culture, particularly if there is no experienced senior management team underneath the CEO, charged with carrying out corporate governance and policy initiatives. The easiest firm to think of in this context is Uber.

If we go back to those leadership books and *Harvard Business Review* articles, we see that they are remarkably the same in the advice they offer to senior managers and to the C-suite: the CEO is asked to delegate responsibility to a senior management team and yet held accountable for gross outcomes. For both, the leader turns into a receiver and evaluator of information shared, rather than a do-er, or a hands-on shaper of the information. In the charged atmosphere of executive decision- making, where anywhere from five to fifteen consequential decisions are made daily, it is easier to accept the information reported than to question it, especially at the executive level. Bonuses in the form of stock or cash make it easier to turn a blind eye to risks that are not completely mitigated, or to control gaps that are reported blandly. If we follow the information trail as it moves from the original identification of the problem, we see that, as we go up the reporting chain, the information becomes increasingly more sanitised from manager to more senior manager; and that the information flow among the three lines of defence begins to fray as well. Not surprisingly, conduct risk is pervasive in today's corporate environment, from the front line to the executive level. Financial loss is often the story of an executive or a manager gone wrong, concealing the true impact of a problem in order to protect bonuses and jobs.

In many firms, we have three people-risk assumptions: that the board is populated with intelligent directors capable of asking hard questions of the CEO; that the CEO hire is a good fit for the company; and that the board will step in and take action if necessary. Though boards of directors may be intelligent, they can only ask hard questions if they get useful reports. (Why was the Wells Fargo board, for example, reassured on employee turnover? Did they get accurate reports with bad explanations? Or what?) If we look at the issue of CEO fit, we see that CEOs put their senior teams together primarily on the basis of their working knowledge. All too often, executives preen in their hires – and end up hiring someone they think is just like herself/himself. The risk of course is that the senior team will simply agree with the executive rather than cause a flap by raising questions.

Directly following on the heels of people risk is process risk – financial loss that stems from flawed, broken or non-existent business processes. An example might be the conversion of detailed identification of serious risk to a dashboard that shows green, yellow or red status, without attaching the detail to the dashboard for further examination. We might see a similar sanitisation upward when reports are prepared for boards of directors.

Having come from one of the largest bank failures in history, I find that I have since then revised my views on why Washington

Mutual failed. Previously, I had placed the failure squarely on the shoulders of a CEO overtaken by hubris, a scholar of Jim Collins books who read and thought extensively about growth and shareholder value. It is only after having spent more time with other banks and back-tracking to detect the operational causes of financial loss that I have begun to see that perhaps the CEO does not always receive the information she/he needs to make the best decision at any given point in time. All the delegation to subordinates leads to the possibility of operational blindness. It is here that there is a real opportunity for the chief risk officer to step forward on behalf of both the board and the CEO.

Selected *ASA News & Notes* Columns

ASA News & Notes is our own in-house newsletter, published monthly since November of 2009, produced by the ASA Institute for Risk and Innovation that continues to offer the latest high level threat analyses and risk assessments on a wide variety of real world issues in order to drive policy and regulatory changes. I have gone back to the end of 2016 to select several columns that align well with the articles and headnotes that comprise the bulk of this volume. Many of them focus on the extraordinary chaos and disruption felt across this country since Donald Trump was elected as president in November of 2016.

Can you spell kakistocracy?
December 2016

The morning after national elections I received an email from my editor at *The Risk Universe* magazine, in which she asked if I would write a reflection for the December issue on risks connected with the election results. I said yes because I thought that with a month's passing I would have a better sense of where the president-elect would be taking us. After all, by then he would have made his cabinet appointments, which would tell us a great deal. I wish I had asked for two months to write the piece because, as you know, several key appointments like that of the Secretary of State have not yet been made, and the list of candidates for the position has gotten longer, not shorter.

From the analysis last week for the magazine, I wanted to lift one of my paragraphs and then say a bit more about it. "Come January, based upon President-elect Trump's statements and the cabinet level nominations that he has made to date, it appears to me that Americans will be citizens of a kakistocracy, which Oxford Dictionaries defines as 'government by the least suitable or competent citizens of a state.' Though I am trying to keep an open mind, it is hard to do so when many cabinet posts are being filled by former military generals or by private sector persons with either no record of public service, or with an attitude that foreshadows dismantling a range of government programs."

The Senate has already provided language in a bill that will be signed by President Obama that waives the requirement that a former military officer be retired for at least seven years before he is appointed to a role normally held by a civilian --Secretary of the Department of Defense -- where oversight of the military is at stake.

Another ominous sign can be read from the transition team's

request of the Department of Energy. From NPR's Jennifer Ludden in a December 9 story: "It wants to know who at the Department of Energy attended domestic and international climate talks. It wants emails about those conferences. It also asks about money spent on loan-guarantee programs for renewable energy. ... The Trump team questionnaire also asks about the Energy Department's role in the Iran nuclear deal, which Trump has called 'stupid.' And it asks for the 20 highest paid employees at the department's national laboratories." At bare minimum, such a request intimidates career-level public servants, and provides still another kind of map of where the administration plans to go.

Several latest examples of kakistocracy: in an interview with Fox News this morning, the president-elect confirmed that he has rejected daily intelligence briefings: "I get it when I need it....I'm, like, a smart person. I don't have to be told the same thing every single day for the next eight years – could be eight years...I don't need that." (Marisa Schultz, *New York Post*, December 11, 2016) Pair this interview with Trump's refusal to believe CIA reports that the Russians interfered with the presidential election, along with his general disdain for the quality of government agencies' intelligence reports and you see what career diplomats and intelligence professionals are up against.

Several of the mid-career students in my course this past quarter wrote their final papers on the post-truth era in which we now find ourselves. Fake news abounds on social media platforms such as Twitter and Facebook, some promulgated by the president-elect, members of his leadership team, or from Breitbart, the syndicated news organization from which the president-elect's strategic advisor comes. Facts are not recognized as facts. Conspiracy stories are favorites of groups who have railed against political correctness. It's not just KKK members parading in their regalia. In this liberal corner of the country, Muslims have been victims of senseless and violent acts, in particular women who cover their heads. Swastikas get painted on buildings, sometimes even on homes. Though the president-elect has said "stop it," his followers feel empowered by the election results, and his words encourage them to make American great again – code words we now see for the most depraved kinds of behavior, including the chants and behaviors we observed at his political rallies.

It will take some time for the other two branches of government to respond, once the inauguration has taken place. Will the Senate confirm all his nominees? Will the high court find itself re-adjudicating old cases, especially in the area of the First and the Fourth Amendments? Women's rights? Immigration? Naturalization? Will the new president resolve the many conflicts of interest in which he finds himself enmeshed? We are in uncharted territory.

Yes, Virginia, we still have three branches of government
February 2017

We have entered the fourth week of the new administration. It would be a relief to report that the White House staff had become more organized and that the most problematic cabinet and staff appointments had resigned, but that will have to wait, I suspect, until even more mistakes have been made. The least stressful way to understand events since January 20th would be watch back episodes of "Saturday Night Live."

We knew while he was campaigning that the president did understand that the Congress is made up of elected representatives. He was quick to tie those up for re-election to his own fate. Though he promised over and over to "drain the swamp" and to "fix Washington" in his campaign, he has instead brought in a significant number of billionaires to his cabinet, and worked hard to keep Congressional Republicans in line to confirm cabinet nominees; and to support his seemingly unending executive orders. This has been accomplished in the most chaotic manner ever seen in the White House, which displays a complete lack of regard for the system of checks and balances from which the federal government works.

We now have a better picture of his view of the judicial branch. Trump may be outraged that two federal courts can stay his immigration ban, causing him to retaliate with tweets that engage in the worst kind of disrespect and name-calling. After such a botched rollout of the immigration ban, he has learned in theory that any executive order should be extremely vetted with the departments they fall to and with members of Congress as well. Staff at the Department of Homeland Security, faced with immediate and unplanned implementation of the ban, found itself relieved days later when the ban was stayed. The Acting Attorney General, a career diplomat, was fired by the president for telling members of the Justice Department that she felt the ban was unenforceable.

The Justice Department (with its new Attorney General confirmed only after these two federal court appeals had been heard) was charged with defending the immigration ban in those courts. Part of the argument they made is that presidential executive orders are "unreviewable" by the courts. The 9th District Court of Appeals, in concurring with the Washington State Solicitor General who argued the plaintiff's case, said of the matter:

*"Instead, the Government has taken the position that the President's decisions about immigration policy, particularly when motivated by national security concerns, are unreviewable, even if those actions potentially contravene constitutional rights and protections. The Government indeed asserts that it violates separation of powers for the judiciary to entertain a constitutional challenge to executive actions such as this one. There is no precedent to support this claimed unreviewability, which runs contrary to the fundamental structure of our constitutional democracy. See Boumediene v. Bush, 553 U.S. 723, 765 (2008) (rejecting the idea that, even by congressional statute, Congress a the Executive could eliminate federal court habeas jurisdiction over enemy combatants, because the "political branches" lack "the power to switch the Constitution on or off at will" [resolution). Within our system, it is the role of the judiciary to interpret the law, a duty that will sometimes require the "of litigation challenging the constitutional authority of one of the three branches." Zivotofsky ex rel.Zivotofsky v. Clinton.566 U.S. 189, 196 (2012) (quoting INS v. Chadha, 462 U.S. 919, 943 (1983)). **We are called upon to perform that duty in this case.** Although our jurisprudence has long counseled deference to the political branches on matters of immigration and national security, neither the Supreme Court nor our court has ever held that courts lack the authority to review executive action in those arenas for compliance with the Constitution."*

One of the president's options now is to draft a new executive order. Another is to appeal the existing 9th court decision to the Supreme Court, given that the appeals court laid down sufficient information in its findings for the Supreme Court to decide if it wishes or needs to hear an appeal. If the president is well-advised at all, it will come as no surprise if the Supreme Court declines to hear the case and let the appeals court finding stay in place. There is no need for him to ask all 29 judges on the 9th District Court of Appeals to determine whether the three judges who made the ruling were correct; the three judges have already offered to have their ruling reviewed by the full district appeals court if the other 26 deem it important.

I started in one place and wish to end in another. There is no doubt that, for many of us, our productivity has been severely compromised by the new administration. No matter what we are in the middle of, we check our mobile devices to see if other troubling programs have been announced, or if there are new executive orders on any given day. I am heartened by the overwhelming number of lawyers who drove to airports to help ensure that rights were respected on those first days before the ban was stayed. I am impressed with politics at the local level, not just here in Seattle but in other major cities as well, where large demonstrations to protest such actions have taken place. That is just the tip of the spear. There is a relatively new attempt to understand how politics work, to figure out how to let your Congressional representative know your views on a wide range of appointments and bills they will be voting on. Finally, more conversations are taking place face to face, not just on social media.

I was overwhelmed by Adam Gopnik's column in the latest issue of *The New Yorker,* which ends thus: "Democratic civilization has turned out to be even more fragile than we imagined; the resources of civil society have turned out to be even deeper than we knew. The battle between these two shaping forces--between the axman assaulting the new growth and the still firm soil and deep roots that support the tree of liberty--will now shape the future of us all."

Next month, I'll plan to take a look at the dismantling of the Dodd-Frank Act.

Learning the hard way how the government works
May 2017

We're evidently in a new stage of political grief – blaming others, be it others who didn't vote as we thought they should, or those who didn't vote at all. We spend hours each day reading bad tweets, watching political commentators trying to find the thread in what's just happened or predicting what they think will happen. We are suckered into many of the same forms of distractibility that the president suffers from. We see cabinet secretaries beginning to dismantle the very agencies or departments they lead. We are comforted by those who agree with us on how terrible things are. Once in a while, we might fire off a letter to our elected representatives, whom neither political party has much confidence in, but mostly we are still in shock over last November's election.

We have the results just in from France's election, and breathe a sigh of relief. We're still watching England, to see just what the Brexit will include. As in this country, the wheels of government turn slowly, which is to be desired at this point in our history.

In just a few months, the president has taken 90 executive actions – executive orders, presidential memoranda, or presidential proclamations -- designed primarily to undo orders or laws made by the previous administration. Proclamations of days, weeks or months are standard fare. Two of the memoranda concern rolling back Dodd-Frank legislation. There have been 32 executive orders covering areas such as travel bans, trade and manufacturing, offshore energy exploration, steel and aluminum dumping, federal powers in education, protecting national lands, Wall Street regulation, reviewing tax regulations, the opioid crisis, climate change protections, and of course the one covering his intention to repeal the Patient Protection and Affordable Care Act.

Never has there been so much zealous focus on repealing and replacing parts of the Affordable Care Act. House Republicans finally managed to produce a mish-mash piece of legislation that on a second try squeaked by (217-213). Despite partying in the Rose Garden to celebrate this success, the bill is still a long way from becoming law. For those not familiar with the process, spending some time on the website votesmart.com might be helpful. From that website we learn that once any bill has been voted on, "If passed, it is then sent to the other chamber unless that chamber already has a similar measure under consideration. If either chamber does not pass the bill then it dies. If the House and Senate pass the same bill then it is sent to the President. If the House and Senate pass different bills they are sent to Conference Committee. Most major legislation goes to a Conference Committee." This will most certainly be the case on the health care bill as it stands right now. When Congress comes back in session, the Senate will take up the legislation it has been sent. The Senate is a different kettle of fish than the House of Representatives, and it will either write a new bill or significantly revise the House bill, sending it to conference committee.

I won't spend much time here on the bill itself, except to say that its becoming law would be catastrophic in several respects, especially for low income citizens and for the power it would send to states to adjust pricing for high risk pools, which is to say that those with pre-existing conditions (and there are many) would most likely not be able to afford the insurance with the surcharge included. There is a fundamental disagreement between Democrats and conservative Republicans on the role of the federal government to ensure health care for all, even though such a change as the new bill proposes will hit many Trump supporters hard.

Getting good information from Republican representatives about what the bill contains is challenging. Evidently many did not ever read the legislation they voted on. (I'd like to note for the record, though, that our congressional representative Dave Reichert voted against the bill. He had received a great deal of input from citizens on the bill).

Moving past finger-pointing or feelings of paralysis, what can one do? Now would be the time to consider your responsibilities as a citizen. Please take the time to write to your senators, and perhaps again to House representatives to express your concerns about this and other pieces of regulation that are under fire at this time. Understand better what is going on in your own community, and resolve to participate more actively. Those who sat out the election because they felt (as 25 percent or so in France did) that neither presidential candidate would pass their sniff test, can now roll up their sleeves and go to work to reform both parties and to consider new ideas, which takes time and energy both. Without such discussions and actual change, our risk exposure actually goes up. There is also a great deal to be done to educate citizens about why they should vote and what difference it does make. Make yourself part of the change you would like to see.

The limits of presidential power
June 2017

In my operational risk seminar this spring, students ranked and then restacked and ranked the top operational risks present in our world. No one was especially pleased with the results, and the top three risks – cyber-threats, global uncertainty, and terrorism – seemed nearly interchangeable, depending upon the month. As we came to the end of the quarter – particularly with the terrorism acts in Manchester, London, and Tehran -- "global uncertainty" seemed to encapsulate the other two risks, particularly when the elections in France and Great Britain are taken into account along with the performance of the U.S. president on his first diplomatic trip abroad.

It's been an anxiety-provoking six months for most of the country. The Fear, Uncertainty & Dread (FUD) machine has been working online round the clock and, as a result, we are spending more time on our smartphones to find the president's latest tweets or to read the latest in a series of executive orders. Our days begin with the news, and often that news is simply more churn, a version of reality television. We wait now to see if the Supreme Court will hear the travel ban case, or simply let the lower court ruling stand. It has taken until this past week for the Senate Intelligence Committee to conduct public hearings that are designed to better understand the Russian intrusion into the last American presidential election and, at the same time, understand whether or not the president and his advisors have colluded or obstructed any of the investigations taking place. This week's set of Senate hearings has caused the House Intelligence Committee to spring back into action, requesting both copies of the Comey memos and any tapes that the president recorded of his conversations with former FBI Director Comey. It is not likely that we will hear from Special Counsel Robert Mueller, who has assembled a team and taken over responsibility for grand jury cases pending on the Russian matter. The work of the special counsel on Russian intervention into our elections may broaden to include considerations around presidential obstruction of justice, but will undoubtedly take much longer than the news cycles to which we have become accustomed. In the meantime, we have to assume that the checks and balances among the three branches of government – together with journalism, the Fourth Estate – will continue to function.

In a provocative article reprinted in the Weekend *Financial Times*, titled "How the Bible Belt Lost God and Found Trump," Gary Silverman quotes Wayne Flynt, a southern history professor who notes a significant change in the Bible Belt population that voted for Trump: "The words of Jesus, as recorded in the Gospels, are less central to their thinking and behavior, he says. Church is less compelling. Marriage is less important. Reading from a severely abridged Bible, their political concerns have narrowed down to abortion and issues involving homosexuality. Their faith, he says, has been put in a president who embodies an unholy trinity of materialism, hedonism and narcissism. Trump's victory, in this sense, is less an expression of the old-time religion than evidence of a move away from it." Later in the article he describes this phenomenon as "a sort of late-stage Christian afterglow."

Trump won 84 percent of white evangelical voters, who approve of the promises he made, whether it was to deny funding to Planned Parenthood, to replace and repeal Obamacare, to put a conservative justice on the Supreme Court, or to bring back jobs that had disappeared when the Environmental Protection Agency and the climate change movement created new jobs for new sources of energy. In a series of executive orders the president has increased the work of the judicial branch. At this time, he still has not found legislative partnership with Republicans in the Congress. Though his version of a health care bill passed on the House side, the Senate is still in the process of writing a new bill which then will go to conference committee. His tax code bill appears to be in a state of paralysis as well. Whether he can persuade Congress to work with him to pass legislation is still up in the air, so we can expect to see more executive orders, some of which will go straight to court.

It is worth noting that, though there are limits on what the president can do without another branch of government, he has managed to redirect and redefine the priorities of many of his departments and agencies. The most obvious examples are the Justice Department and the Department of Homeland Security (DHS). For DHS, a priority has been placed on sweeping up illegal immigrants and, though the priority is on those illegal immigrants who have committed crimes, no one is being careful to only sweep criminal immigrants. For the Justice Department, the significant work done by the prior administration on police reform has been swept away; and we now see an emphasis on longer jail sentences. The Justice Department is also a victim of the Russian investigation, so we will be treated next week to the spectacle of the Attorney General testifying before the Senate Intelligence Committee on his contacts with Russian officials.

The press has never been as maligned as they have been by this president. Insults and allegations of "fake news" are part of an incendiary tool kit to undo the news as we understand it and to boost the president's standing in the evangelical community. If you are not already subscribing to one or more of our great American newspapers, please consider doing so. You may also wish to consider a donation to the Committee to Protect Journalists, whose span is global.

Last word goes to Charles P. Pierce in *Esquire*: "People talk about it matter-of-factly, the way they talk about rain when dark clouds gather over the monuments by the river. They also talk about it in whispers while every institution of democratic government screams for help. The government of the United States is in the hands of feckless time-servers and coat-holders at one end of Pennsylvania Avenue, and in the hands of an unpredictable and perilous clown show at the other. It is an altogether remarkable, if terrifying place to be as summer comes on."

The stakes have never been higher
August 2017

My summer reading has focused primarily on two important books. The first, from Richard A. Clarke and R.P. Eddy, is *Warnings: Finding Cassandras to Stop Catastrophes*. I recommend it highly. Using examples, the authors lay out four components of what they call "the Cassandra Coefficient" – a grid that horizontally reads as "The Warning," then "The Decision Maker," then "The Cassandra," and finally "The Critics." Factors that read vertically under, for instance, "The Warning," include response availability, initial occurrence syndrome, erroneous consensus, magnitude overload, outlandishness and invisible obvious. There are also seven types of "The Cassandra:" a proven technical expert, an off-putting personality, a data-driven analyst, an orthogonal thinker, questioners, and a Cassandra with a sense of personal responsibility. And, of course, there are false Cassandras.

There are 16 historic events analyzed in the book. For me, the most poignant chapter was on the rise of ISIS, with emphasis on Syria. The Cassandra identified was Robert Ford, the Arabist, who was unable to persuade the cautious Obama administration over a long period of time of what he saw on the ground and through his Foreign Service experience in most Arab countries. As a result of Obama's long view of the Mideast and his distaste for its wars, the president as decision maker did not follow the advice of his expert, and the situation in Syria has played out exactly as Ambassador Ford predicted. "The decision maker, in this case President Obama, saw the immediate situation in a larger context and believed the benefits of acting were outweighed by the risks and perhaps the opportunity costs." (71)

I wish that the discussion occurring inside government today was as nuanced as that on the Mideast or North Korea during the Obama administration. Instead we are living with a president who barely speaks in complete sentences, who reacts rather than thinks. Last week, I had just read Mark Bowden's piece outlining our four North Korea options in *The Atlantic*. I thought I would be examining what happens when confrontations between countries are treated as high stakes wrestling matches with rhetorical threats better left to reality television than to the real world. It may still be the case that North Korea will act upon its threats and send missiles toward Guam by the middle of this month, and that our military will be faced with real time testing of a system designed to bring down such missiles. I have confidence in the military leaders that now surround the president, but no confidence in the president. His rhetoric does not align with the severity of the situation. There is a very large gap between what he says and what his chief of staff and cabinet members say. It's clear that we have been deploying cyber tools where some past tests are concerned -- software problems and faulty parts in the supply chain come to mind -- and toward that end, here is my second book recommendation: Alexander Klimberg's *The Darkening Web: The War for Cyberspace*. Klimberg uses both historic examples and sharp argument to enumerate the threats, which range from the destruction of this country's critical infrastructure to an Orwellian view of the loss of privacy and freedom of expression. I keep reading this book because, despite the gutting of the government offices of science and technology and an apparent lack of understanding at the highest levels of government of what cyber tools deployed by Russians have wrought, this is the world today. You might wish to look also at Jared Cohen's opinion piece, "How to Prevent a CyberWar," (*New York Times*, August 12, 2017) The work he proposes can and should go on, with or without the current administration.

Finally, who would have thought that the North Korea situation would be nearly eclipsed in the news by the tragic events in Charlottesville, home of the University of Virginia? Not in my lifetime have I seen members of white supremacists and Nazi groups, including the Ku Klux Klan, gather en masse with hoods and torches on a Friday evening, and in violent assault, with and without hoods but with weapons, the next day. Predictably, we have a presidential statement on Saturday's events that does not even allude to the actual situation, and replies upon the most platitudinous rhetoric: "No matter our color, creed, religion or political party, we are ALL AMERICANS FIRST." Republican and Democratic members of Congress have suggested the president harshly condemn the white supremacists, with some suggesting they fought the Nazis in World War II, and were willing to re-enlist in that fight again. It is clear that the president will not directly condemn his own supporters using his usual tweets. He has left it to his staff to produce statements that try to paint his tweets as strategic, but it is Former KKK leader David Duke who makes clear the connection: "I would recommend you take a good look in the mirror & remember it was White Americans who put you in the presidency, not radical leftists," and at the same time complains about the platitudes: "So, after decades of White Americans being targeted for discriminated & anti-White hatred, we come together as a people, and you attack us?"

I began by saying that the stakes have never been higher. The dark cultural underbelly of this country is now visible, not merely because we have smartphones and can document it, but also because we have a leader who thrives on stirring things up, whether North Korea, China, and Venezuela – while he ignores both Russia and the larger threats to this country, while we try to move past injustice, inequity and moral meltdown toward what the founders called a more perfect union. Rhetoric matters.

America as a killing field
October 2017

"A well regulated Militia, being necessary to the security of a free State, the right of the people to keep and bear Arms, shall not be infringed."

-- Second Amendment, U.S. Constitution, ratified 1791.

In the past month, our screens have been overwhelmed with stories of images of misery, injury and death – first from three devastating hurricanes from which it will take years to recover and to rebuild both homes and infrastructure; and more recently, from indelible images of the largest mass shooting in modern U.S. history. Though not all the numbers are in yet for Puerto Rico, we lost at least 137 people in those three hurricanes; and another 58 in the Las Vegas shooting.

All four events have caused unlimited pain and deprivation, but here I'd like to speak out against the most powerful lobby in the United States working once again to keep us from answering certain questions and amending current gun laws or creating a new one, and what we might do about it.

How is it that there is no national registry of firearms that would count and register as an anomaly the purchase of a large number of weapons in a short period of time? Though machine guns (automatic weapons) were banned from sale to citizens in 1986, an adaptive hardware kit (a bump stock kit) is sold freely that converts a semi-automatic to fire as an automatic weapon. We read that most police forces endorse the use of background checks, yet background checks are not performed on all buyers across all sales venues on the sale of firearms using (for example) the FBI database, which is the largest amalgamation of information available to law enforcement today. The ironies abound, even as the National Rifle Association (NRA) has created a powerful lobby to keep Congressional representatives voting their way by brainwashing gun owners to state as fact that stronger gun control measures will result in the government taking guns away from the people.

It's hard to remember that in the 1700s, the amendment was written just after the Revolutionary War, when militias were the means by which the colonists protected themselves against British soldiers, who wanted not only to take away their arms but also to take up residence in their homes. Today our "well regulated Militia" includes local, state and federal law enforcement, as well as over 2,000,000 paid members of the armed forces: projected for 2017 are 1,281,900 people in active duty end strength, with an additional 801,200 people in the seven reserve components. All these members are armed on our behalf.

Yes, we have some gun laws on the books, but we must go further. I am not suggesting an end to civilian gun ownership, but rather that we treat gun ownership like we treat driving a car or flying an airplane: that a certain amount of education/ actual training be required to own a gun that would result in a training certificate so that a weapon could be purchased. A universal background check would take place at point of sale, culminating in the registration of weapons and certificates, not so they can be taxed, but rather so gun ownership can be tracked and the movement of weapons among owners is known. The fact that even this is opposed by the most extreme opponents of any limitation reflects a deep and deeply troubling distrust of civil government itself.

We remember the large mass shooting events, but roughly 93 people die from guns on an average day in the United States. We need to elect Congressional representatives willing to stand up to the NRA, and able to explain to voters exactly what they stand for where gun controls are concerned. If we had a gun registry in place, then it is entirely possible that the Las Vegas gunman would have stood out because of the 33 weapons (and the types of weapons they were) that he purchased in the twelve months.

These recommendations are not new, nor are they radical. Writing for the majority of the Supreme Court in 2008, the late Justice Antonin Scalia said: "Like most rights, the right secured by the Second Amendment is not unlimited...nothing in our opinion should be taken to cast doubt on longstanding prohibitions on the possession of firearms by felons and the mentally ill, or laws forbidding the carrying of firearms in sensitive places such as schools and government buildings, or laws imposing conditions and qualifications on the commercial sale of arms."

Lest we are too preoccupied to care deeply on this matter, here are similar events that might ring a bell and inspire you to vote, and to contact Congressional representatives supported by the NRA: the Orlando nightclub (49 dead, 58 wounded); Virginia Tech (32 dead, 17 wounded) and Sandy Hook Elementary School (26 dead, 2 wounded). These are only the most memorable in recent history. Haven't we had enough? Isn't it time to act?

Our darkest hour is still ahead
January 2018

Just like that, we are in a new year. From a risk management perspective, it's difficult to miss the signs that warn us that our democratic form of government is under attack. Last week, former FBI director James Comey tweeted: "Where are the voices of all the leaders who know an independent Department of Justice and FBI are essential to our liberty? 'You are not only responsible for what you say, but also for what you do not say.'— Martin Luther"

It is not just that the size of the government has been reduced intentionally. It is not just that many cabinet level appointees are unqualified for public service. It is not only that our government policies have been revised or in some cases re-interpreted or eliminated. Similarities to conditions in Germany that led to the rise of Hitler are hard to miss – the nationalistic, boastful tone; the harsh and unrelenting attacks on a free press as "fake news;" the key roles that members of the military play in the current administration; the endless insults and sparring with other countries; the deaf ear turned to hate speech; and the pitiful, narcissistic, and whiny tweets from the nation's highest elected official.

Each winter when I teach a graduate level course in information ethics and policy, we begin with a reading out loud of both the Declaration of Independence and the Bill of Rights. There is a gap of some years between when the Declaration of Independence (1776) and the U.S. Constitution (1787) were enacted, and another gap before we have the first amendments to the Constitution (1789). Nonetheless, the elevated language and the breadth of vision found in all three documents remind us of the ambition and determination of the Founding Fathers. The

Declaration is, as Danielle Allen reminds us, a first example of democratic writing. The Constitution lays out the structure and powers of the federal government, including its three branches and the related principles of "separation of powers" – that each branch operates independently – and the other of "checks and balances" -- to prevent too much of a concentration of power in any one branch. The President, for example, can veto Congress' bills. The Supreme Court can declare a law written by Congress as unconstitutional; and Congress can impeach the president and judges.

What are now the first ten amendments – our Bill of Rights – document what the government cannot do and, in several cases, what it must do. It is on the Bill of Rights that students spent most time last Friday evening. Several hold green cards to work in this country, and were able to describe how conditions have changed for them in the past year. One student noted that, in the past, when you were in this country, you were afforded the same rights as citizens have, including a presumption of innocence. That is no longer the case. International students can expect to be stopped, investigated, and sometimes harassed, and not just during a border crossing. Another student noted that he carried his papers with him at all times to avoid detention. These are painful perspectives for those of us who enjoy the full benefits of citizenship and the rule of law. How much our federal government has changed this past year in terms of both convention and continuity of government!

State attorneys general have challenged a range of policies and procedures designed to crack down on "aliens." I know that the Supreme Court will eventually rule upon the modified immigration law that is now in place, but it takes time for appeals to move through the lower courts. Since our Supreme Court justices are mindful of the intentions of the authors of the Constitution and its amendments, I hope they will remember when it is time to rule that all those who signed the three documents that provide the basis for our form of government were themselves immigrants.

Focusing on these three documents at the same time as I began to read *Fire and Fury: Inside the Trump White House* and after I had seen "Darkest Hour" over the holidays was instructive. I have become more determined to begin to act now rather than simply observe and comment on events as history is made. We need to register voters and to convince registered voters to cast their ballots. It is the only way to restore more of a balance among the three branches of government, which are each saturated today with Trump majorities in the form of Enthusiasts, Impressionables, Sycophants and Ignoramuses.

In her close reading of the Declaration of Independence, Danielle Allen reminds us of the power of language and ideas: The achievement of political equality requires, among other things, the empowerment of human beings as language-using creatures." [*Our Declaration: A Reading of the Declaration of Independence in Defense of Equality*]

Looking toward a more just society
February 2018

"To ask whether a society is just is to ask how it distributes the things we prize – income and wealth, duties and rights, powers and opportunities, offices and honors. A just society distributes these goods in the right way: it gives each person his or her due. The hard questions begin when we ask what persons are due, and why." (Michael J. Sandel. "Doing the Right Thing" in *Justice*, 2009)

It's been a long couple of weeks, as our president attempted gravitas in his State of the Union address on January 30, having signed into law the tax reform bill on December 22, 2017. His address was billed as an inclusive address, one that would reach across the aisle, and move the country forward. By the time he spoke, because of a failure to provide for DACA recipients in the budget bill, the federal government had already been shut down once (January 20-22), and Congress was working on a very short leash to agree and then pass a budget, with a commitment to consideration of a DACA bill before early March. The stakes changed in his State of the Union address, however. He suggested that Congress would not take up the DACA issue without also changing current immigration policy – in particular around family-based immigration ("chain migration") and the current lottery provisions – and providing funds for a border wall along Mexico. The address made clear that the president is looking for a quid pro quo – dreamers for tougher, more restrictive policies and funding for his border wall. He has indicated he is open to including persons not currently enrolled in DACA – which would mean that an estimated 2.14 million to be eligible for conditional legal status and 1.73 million to qualify for lawful permanent residence status, per the legislation proposed by Senators Graham and Durbin.

Like many of the president's actions, what looks like a just approach to the dreamers has long-term, negative consequences on federal immigration policy, reminding us of the characterizations coming out of the White House of certain countries as "shitholes" and of those not yet signed up for DACA as either scared or "too lazy to get off their asses." Just as the major tax cuts go to the very wealthy in this country, the administration favors immigrants from well-off, non-Muslim countries like Norway. Tax reform significantly benefits only the wealthiest among us, and does not even pretend to be a pathway to a more just society.

The budget finally signed by the president on February 9th did not contain a DACA or immigration policy element. Rather it played catch up on pressing issues: it "set up a two-year, $300 billion boost in spending on military and domestic programs. It ... also extend[ed] the debt ceiling, authorize[d] nearly $90 billion more in aid for last year's string of natural disasters, ... funding to fight the opioid crisis and extend the popular Children's Health Insurance Program for an additional four years." (CNBC) Nothing more need be said here about whether or not such a budget will drive sufficient revenues to afford the tax cuts authorized in December. We still have to deal with DACA and immigration policy and the border wall by early March. Ironically, of all the president's endorsements, dealing with DACA recipients fairly move us toward two of the approaches for a better societal distribution of goods that Sandel discusses in Justice: duties and rights; and powers and opportunities.

At the same time that the Special Counsel moves forward on his investigation, we see an increasing number of pointers to obstruction of justice. Not just in the president's past actions, tweets and speeches to his base, but also in the behind-the-scenes pressure being put on both the Department of Justice and the FBI, both of whom have seen an increasing number of resignations at senior levels. In total, the president has himself personally assaulted the notion of a just society, often in speech that I believe the Supreme Court would consider unprotected by the First Amendment. Because he behaves and speaks in such a manner, his followers feel free to also speak in public gatherings in the same way. In 1942, the Supreme Court of the United States declared "fighting words" to be unprotected – and defined them as "words by the very utterance inflict injury or tend to incite an immediate breach of the peace." If he is not already at this state, he is very close.

His behavior reminds us that, in our pursuit of a just society we must be careful not to "become what we behold." (William Blake) I was reminded of this here in Seattle yesterday, when a Patriots Prayer rally on the University of Washington campus brought out twice its number in counter-protesters, who were certainly able to drown out the rally with shouted chants, including some who covered their faces while looking for action. I remember earlier days, where standing silently in protest while bearing witness led to actual change because the media could report the content of such speeches rather than make violence and altercations the focus of the story.. We need to find a balance between bearing witness and enacting change that will lead to a more just society.

DHS is making a list and checking it twice
April 2018

"No experiment can be more interesting than that we are now trying, and which we trust will end in establishing the fact, that man may be governed by reason and truth. Our first object should therefore be, to leave open to him all the avenues to truth. The most effectual hitherto found, is the freedom of the press. It is, therefore, the first shut up by those who fear the investigation of their actions."

–Thomas Jefferson

"We are not afraid to entrust the American people with unpleasant facts, foreign ideas, alien philosophies, and competitive values."

–John F. Kennedy

"Freedom of conscience, of education, of speech, of assembly are among the very fundamentals of democracy and all of them would be nullified should freedom of the press ever be successfully challenged."

–Franklin D. Roosevelt

The Department of Homeland Security (DHS) has launched a bid request to create a "media monitoring services," describing a plan to identify, then gather and monitor professional journalists and "top media influencers" – from the RFI, we learn that DHS will track more than 290,000 news sources around the world as well as social media in over 100 languages (with immediate translation into English). In the bid's statement of work, we learn that the successful bidder will have created "24/7 access to a password protected, media influencer database, including journalists, editors, correspondents, social media influencers, bloggers, etc." so as to "identify any and all media coverage related to the Department of Homeland Security or a particular event." (FedBizOpps Solicitation Number: RNBO-18-00041)

For those who are unfamiliar with DHS except in a very general sense, the department includes these agencies, whose media coverage would presumably be included: U.S. Customs and Border Protection; U.S. Citizenship and Immigration Services; U.S. Coast Guard; FEMA; the Secret Service; U.S. Immigration and Customs Enforcement (ICE); and the Transportation Security Administration (TSA). Because of the current administration's executive orders, as for instance on the revised travel ban, and a heightened desire by the administration to toughen existing immigration laws and hire thousands of additional border agents, one must presume that the administration will be "monitoring" for a reason. I say that despite the tweet of the DHS Press Secretary Tyler Q. Houlton on April 7: *"Despite what some reporters may suggest, this is nothing more than the standard practice of monitoring current events in the media. Any suggestion otherwise is fit for tin foil hat wearing, black helicopter conspiracy theorists."* My colleague Sean Costigan tweeted back: *"Dear DHS, If you had simply asked a librarian you would have learned that BBC Monitoring Services does what you seem to want, without the worries over ruining our rights..."*

I have often written about DHS, one or more of its agencies. As we go to press, Forbes reports that there are at least seven companies planning to bid on this project. I will let the quotes from Jefferson. Kennedy and Roosevelt speak for themselves, and for the concern that many of us media commentators have on this move from a cabinet department that has a disproportionate amount of influence and power with the president. Though the aim stated is to monitor professional media coverage, we have seen in the past how such scrutiny can lead to gross violations of reporters' rights, which leads me to the other large piece of our public infrastructure that I wanted to discuss this month.

On Tuesday, Facebook CEO Mark Zuckerberg will begin two days of Congressional testimony. Like all CEOs compelled to appear in front of one or more Congressional committees, he will first of all appear abject and apologetic for the gross invasions of Facebook users' privacy. He will have three or four steps to point to that he and his teams are preparing to deploy in light of the Cambridge Analytica breach. To my mind, however, he has already announced the largest single change that will be deployed: the adoption of the Global Data Protection Regulation (GDPR), which is being rolled out by the European Union in May of this year. Among the rights that GDPR guarantees to data subjects are the right to notification (breach notification within 72 hours); the right to access (is the data being collected and how?); the right to data erasure (also known as "right to be forgotten"); the right to data portability (ability of the subject to receive the data and move his/her data to another controller); and privacy by design (the responsibility to collect and hold only the minimum amount of data required and to provide access only to same). Adopting GDPR is a logical step for multinational companies like Facebook, Twitter and Google because maintaining two standards (U.S. and E.U.) would be too costly, given the sheer volume of data and ensuring that proper protocols are in place when data crosses borders.

Ironically, if the new DHS Media Monitoring Services proceeds, the winning bidder for this global tracking system will have to struggle with all the challenges that GDPR brings to data collection across borders --where the rights of the user are paramount, and when data ownership is a fundamental right— and that will include respecting the rights of a free press as well as the rights of social media users.

Reconsidering risk
June 2018

It is just a year ago that the London-based magazine, *The Risk Universe*, shut down its operation. I had written quarterly for the magazine for five years. Looking back upon the articles, I could see that each was still relevant to any discussion of operational risk. I asked and received permission from publisher Mike Finlay to reprint the articles in a book, with head notes for each of the articles to discuss changes in risk exposure and governance, as well as the ever-changing role of regulators. I am finishing the book this summer. I am considering the addition of several of my columns from this newsletter where I have written on the breakdown of our usual governance processes and the increase in operational risk since January 21, 2017, when Donald Trump became president of the United States.

Any list of breakdowns is too long to publish here, but I'd like to focus on several domestic issues at the heart of governance and its attendant risks. Mass shootings have become more deadly and this year they may have become more frequent. From Grant Duwe in *Politico*, October of 2017: "There is, by now, a familiar script to it all: A mass public shooting, followed by waves of grief and outrage, then calls for gun control on the one hand and harrumphing about politicizing tragedies on the other. The news stories and statements by political leaders write themselves, with only the location, name of the shooter and number of casualties changing. It all seems so routine."

Of late, school shootings seem to be on the rise. There have been at least 23 school shootings this year. Often the shooter has spent hours pouring over older events like the Columbine school shootings in 1999 or the Sandy Hook school shootings in 2016. The current political climate is not helpful: right wing broadcasters suggest the government is coming to take away guns, adding pressure to an already toxic and fragile situation. Some even suggest that Sandy Hook is a false flag, a covert deceptive operation by the federal government, designed so that the Second Amendment right to bear arms will be taken away.

The familiar script that Duwe discusses in his article is being modified somewhat by the #neveragain movement led by students from Margery Stoneman Douglas High School and joined by thousands of middle and high school students from across the nation. Their focus is on registering voters and confronting elected public officials to revise our gun control laws. In this effort, they are up against the most powerful congressional lobby (with the possible exception of the banking lobby), the National Rifle Association (NRA), who wants to point the cause of such shootings elsewhere than guns. It is too early to tell whether voter turnout will be higher, or whether these students and others who stand with them, will persuade younger voters to actually vote in November. Pew estimates millennials (ages 18-35) have the lowest voter turnout, but rival Baby Boomers in size: 31% of the possible vote. Certainly the #neveragain movement will be speaking to them, but it is important to note that the movement is focused on registering persons just now turning 18 years of age. We could see significant change in the fall in both the Senate and the House of Representatives, and certainly at the local level as well.

Matters are not so straightforward where the separation of children from their asylum-seeking parents by U.S. Immigration and Customs Enforcement (ICE) officers. From Michelle Chen in The Nation, June 8, 2018: "They arrive at the border with nothing, stripped of their money, their homes and often, their dignity. Now the United States is robbing them of the one thing they've miraculously clung to through their journey: each other. President Trump's new "zero tolerance" immigration policy aims at 'taking back' the country by taking children from parents. About 700 families have in recent months been systematically separated, with children being separated from parents—even when families could legitimately apply for asylum, and even when doing so puts already terrorized families at even greater risk."

The inhumane plan developed by the administration is an outgrowth of the growing power of ICE during Bush and Obama administrations. Trump's plans include handling up to "11,000 isolated migrant children in federal immigration shelters and military bases." (Chen)

The ACLU recently documented hundreds of incidents in recent years of detained children suffering physical or sexual violence, or being denied medical care and food. Now mothers and kids will be left even more isolated, incarcerated separately; activists say some family members might even be deported while others remain trapped in the United States—turning refugee kids into immigration orphans. (Chen)

Congress has not been able to move any form of legislation on the Dreamers, much less effectively protest this new zero tolerance policy that ratchets up existing powers of ICE with the cooperation of the Department of Justice. Public officials in Washington State (and other states) are reviewing the policy to see if there are grounds to appeal.

I believe the answer can only be found in one place while the current administration is still in power, and that is in the power of the ballot box, the responsibility (and privilege) we all have to vote. The third branch of government, the Supreme Court, may rule on a case that could work its way up, but the November elections are probably closer than a favorable Supreme Court decision.

I am out of time and space, so will only allude to the governance shambles being made on international diplomatic fronts. Diplomacy is being conducted by bluster and insult. As if the G7 Summit behavior were not enough, today we will all be watching the crapshoot between the president and North Korean president Kim Jong-un.

Annie Searle is a full-time faculty lecturer on operational risk as well as on information ethics, policy and law at the University of Washington's Information School, and is the faculty adviser for the University of Washington's ISACA chapter. She is also principal of ASA Risk Consultants, an independent consulting and research firm that helps critical infrastructure companies identify and manage operational risk. Searle is the author of the popular book *Advice From A Risk Detective*. Her ASA Institute for Research and Innovation has published four volumes of research notes on operational risk events and issues in a series called *Reflections on Risk*. Searle authored the second chapter -- "How Does Conduct Risk Manifest and What Are Its Root Causes?" -- of *Conduct Risk: A Practitioner's Guide*, edited by Peter Haines and published by Risk Books of London in 2016. She was inducted into the Hall of Fame for the International Network of Women in Emergency Management and Homeland Security in 2011; and is a lifetime member of the Institute of American Entrepreneurs. Prior to founding ASA in 2009, Searle spent ten years at Washington Mutual Bank as a divisional executive. Her previous careers include public television, the visual arts, and technology. She is an avid gardener, a novice watercolorist, and longtime photographer.

www.ingramcontent.com/pod-product-compliance
Lightning Source LLC
Chambersburg PA
CBHW060611200326
41521CB00007B/735